The Next Level

A Guide for Emerging Leaders

Gina Lucente-Cole

Speak It To Book
www.speakittobook.com

The Next Level / Gina Lucente-Cole
ISBN-13: 978-1-952602-09-2

This book is dedicated to my loving husband, Bob, who supports me and believes in me. I could not have written this book without you. It is also dedicated to my children, Bridget and Alex, who teach me new things every day.

CONTENTS

Who Is the Boss of Your Career? It's Up to You

You are the boss of your career. If you are reading this, you want success. Perhaps you already are successful in some areas, but you want more. You want to keep developing and growing in your role, specialty, organization, or industry. You've tried working harder, but that isn't paying off like it used to. Now you are nervous that you have hit a plateau or are stuck.

You are highly capable, and you bring your skills to your job. Your ability to deliver results has gotten you where you are, but the gap is widening. The things you are being asked to do are becoming more complicated. You've been elevated; however, you still perceive that a gap exists between you and other leaders. The environment around you is evolving, and you feel as if you are just able to keep up, but you aren't sure why you feel this way.

Perhaps you've indeed hit a plateau or even a slowdown. You don't want to get left behind, but you aren't sure what to do to catch up.

You can become the boss of your own career. Just

because you want something doesn't mean that you're willing to do the work to get it or that you're equipped to obtain it. Allow me to help you take charge of your career and close the gap.

The Need to Evolve

Careers today function very differently from how they did in the past. We've left the Industrial Age and now live in the Information Age. You've likely heard the term "knowledge worker," which was first coined by Peter Drucker in 1959.[1] This term refers to a person whose job centers around using information to make decisions and take action. Chances are high that you are one of the workers who use theoretical and analytical knowledge to develop products and services. Your mindset and your approach must reflect what is effective in an Information Age economy.

Today's workforce has the least amount of free time in recent history, **putting in longer hours than at any other time since that data has been tracked.**[2] According to *Harvard Business Review*, the psychological and physical problems of burned-out employees cost an estimated $125 billion to $190 billion a year in healthcare spending in the United States.[3]

What can you do to make sure that your effort at work provides the best results for your professional development and contributes to achieving organizational goals? How can you know what the most important things to focus on are when everything feels urgent and like it requires an immediate response?

As professionals struggle to find balance and productivity, they are dealing with a paradox that David Allen, the author of *Getting Things Done: The Art of Stress-Free Productivity*, describes as "The better you get, the better you'd better get!"[4] This quote refers to the fact that as professionals improve, they will be given more responsibilities that they need to master.

In my experience as a leadership skills trainer and executive coach, I have noticed the following segmentation among emerging and rising leaders in organizations:

- Highly skilled people who leverage their abilities and create their own opportunities

- People who have high potential but coast through work because they aren't challenged

- Accomplished people who have plateaued and are unsure about how to improve their situation

The last group exists because the company they work for or the culture they work in has evolved faster than they have. I will discuss this topic in more detail later in the book.

This book is not for the seasoned executive nearing retirement. It's for emerging and rising leaders who realize that in order to succeed, they need to evolve and adapt. These professionals are finding themselves in increasingly more impactful roles with additional responsibility for business results and leading people.

Oftentimes these people are held back by their fears. They are afraid of falling short of other people's expectations of them. They have seen the gap that exists between where they are and where their high-performing colleagues are. While they are willing to make a change so they can cross over the line of success, they don't know how to move themselves forward. They've run out of tools to navigate their work and feel lost in a space where they used to feel more than capable.

These professionals realize that if things don't change,

they eventually won't be considered for the best projects or new assignments. They are afraid of losing status. They may have employees who report to them on an organizational chart but don't follow their lead very well. They wonder how much longer it will be before they are passed over for new opportunities.

If you've tried everything you know to do and are still searching for the answer, that means you have hope. You haven't given up. You are willing to learn, apply what you learn, and change. *You* are the person I wrote this book for. I can't help you if you've given up on yourself. The good news is that I know you haven't given up on yourself because if you had, you wouldn't be reading a book titled *The Next Level* now, right?

You are a professional who chooses to leverage your skills and talents and make the most of your career. You have a desire to be successful, and you understand that while satisfaction and fulfillment may not come easy, they are worth pursuing. You want to be the example others can follow. You want to exude positivity and happiness.

If I just described you, then congratulations. You have what it takes to get to *the next level*!

Becoming More Valuable

Now that we've talked about you, there are a few things you should know about me. For the past twenty years, I've been helping leaders and managers in organizations to gain the skills they need to take their careers to the next level. Through speaking, writing, conducting webinars, and facilitating workshops, I've impacted *thousands* of emerging and rising leaders and armed them with new knowledge that can impact their careers in significant ways. I've been supporting professionals with honest advice and practical encouragement ever since they entered the workforce, and the main piece of advice I give them is about structure.

This book will teach you the skills and framework to make you more valuable at work and get you to the next level. I'll explain the actions you should take to accelerate your career and what pitfalls to avoid. If you apply what I teach in the way that I teach it, you'll be empowered with the resources you need to further own your personal and professional development. At the end of every chapter, you'll find a workbook section. *Do not* skip those sections. Think of them as the tools you need to apply the knowledge you are gaining to your *already successful* career.

I fully believe that you can reach the next level to become an emerging and rising leader. This book will show you how, and you can inspire others to do the same.

Let's get started.

Note: This book was authored before the international impact of COVID-19 in early 2020. For bonus material related to leading in the "next normal" after the pandemic, please go to ProminaAdvisors.com.

Part One:
Your Role As an Employee

CHAPTER ONE

Take Initiative

Most people tend to assume that the world operates within a clear set of boundaries. We may suppose that organizations function with efficiency and have procedures and processes, that employees have defined roles, and that decisions are made with clear boundaries and input from the appropriate people. We then take this mindset into our jobs as employees of these organizations and assume that our roles are deliberately designed (during the interview process, this may or may not be evident), that the employer will move us along at the proper pace, and that we can work hard and get promoted.

The reality, however, is that most organizations are not this structured and don't function seamlessly. Businesses are often on the defensive more than the offensive, more reactive than proactive, and your employer is not going to lay a clear path of advancement for you. Employers are much too busy putting out fires and doing what is needed to track key metrics and hit their large business targets.

Initiative should come from you. Notice the work that you are drawn to and that you find interesting and engaging. The sooner you embrace this, the sooner you will advance.

You Are a Brand

Fast Company said it best in their 1997 article "The Brand Called You."[5] They introduced a progressive notion way ahead of its time: "We are CEOs of our own companies: Me Inc. To be in business today, our most important job is to be head marketer for the brand called You."

This is good advice.

You are not an employee of such-and-such organization. *You are your own brand.* You're an independent agent, a hired-out service provider, who happens to have one primary client (your employer), work their hours (sometimes in the office, other times remotely), and provide their outputs, ideas, and solutions.

You may have benefits, a salary, and interpersonal relationships. Your LinkedIn bio probably even says that you are someone's employee, but the reality is that you're on your own. You are the person in charge of your career path. You don't have to do it alone, but the onus is on you to take charge and shape your own career path and plan.

There are two common errors professionals make in their approach to career growth. The first error is that they make decisions about their careers with a focus on ten years in the future. It is valuable, and even inspiring, to have a long-term vision of what success means for you, but an over-defined and inflexible plan will not serve you well. To paraphrase the nineteenth-century strategist Helmuth von Moltke, "No plan survives first contact with the enemy."[6]

The second common error is that there is a lack of focus on gaining breadth and depth of experience. It is a balance between honing your skills in your discipline or area and reaching wider for work and experiences that help to round out your skills. These opportunities come with additional time and effort on your part and may include volunteering for a cross-functional initiative at work, beta-testing a new product or app for the research and development group, or taking a day off to help on the organization's community service project. Your focus should be on doing work in the short term that evolves over time into results. Do your work, get feedback, adjust as necessary, and keep delivering.

You won't be serving yourself by drifting along with little or no focus. A path to advancement isn't going to fall into your lap. You need to fight for it, earn it, and make it happen.

You need to take initiative.

Situational Awareness

I've seen people experience a light-bulb moment that changes their perspective. They realize that the more they take initiative in different disciplines and areas that interest and appeal to them, the more their work becomes individualized and tailored to their skill sets. That may sound like a paradox, but let's explore this notion. People who sit back and wait for opportunities often get stuck with a docket of work that isn't interesting to them and drains their energy. As a result, they are unmotivated to do the work.

Conversely, people who take the initiative to build their own workloads shine more. They succeed faster. They're happier and feel that their work makes a difference. Please note that although happiness at work is important, you should not expect that you will enjoy 100% of your work tasks and projects. You will be required to do some work that you think is dull, uninspiring, or a waste of your talent. We all have projects and responsibilities that we wish we could simply ignore, but we must do them anyway. Even if you aren't interested in the quarterly budget report, for instance, you still must bring your best self to the task, play nice with your colleagues and teammates, and support the broader organizational goals.

One of the first steps toward self-initiative is to have situational awareness. This is the ability to assess what is going on in any given situation. In everyday speak, it's the ability to read the room. You need to know whom you're dealing with, who has decision-making power, who influences, and who moves the work forward. A high level of situational awareness can help you to achieve your goals because you'll know whom to impress, whom to befriend as an ally, and whom to be wary of.

If you want to get things done and have sway at work, there are four different types of people that you need to be aware of in the workforce.

1. The Approver is the person who can approve your ideas and grant you permission or resources. He or she may approve assignments to projects, control funding or budgets, or set the work direction and priorities.

2. The Gatekeeper is the person who has the credentials or requirements needed to allow your idea to pass through the chain of command or provide access to resources or tools you need to get things done.

3. The Subject Matter Expert is a person who has depth of knowledge in a particular area. This could be someone on your team or even in another department. This is a person you want to befriend because he or she can offer skills and knowledge completely different from your own and can help to move your work forward by providing expertise or insights.

4. The Naysayer is the person who is always finding the holes in an idea. Naysayers can be both beneficial and detrimental. You will want to avoid detrimental naysayers, as they tend to put down any idea that didn't come from them. At the same time, you'll want to befriend beneficial naysayers. These people can pre-assess your ideas, providing valuable insight into any deficiencies or issues with your proposed plans. One effective approach is to ask the naysayer to review your project and "poke holes in it" or point out what you may have missed.

To know these different types of people, you must branch out. You have to explore other departments within your organization and dare to get involved. You must ask questions and seek to understand the unique areas of expertise being represented at work. Technology, sales, marketing, research and development, purchasing, client services, distribution—these are just some of the departments in which you should form a relationship with one or more colleagues.

Once you develop those relationships and have won over others by delivering quality work and supporting your team and colleagues, you will have a clearer path forward.

A Blank Canvas

There are many sources of advice about leadership. I enjoy books, blogs, and podcasts that explore all the facets of the topic, but I think the simplest way to define leadership is as the ability to inspire others to act. When it comes to being a leader, I believe a key aspect that is often overlooked.

A *Harvard Business School* article emphasizes that this key to true leadership "lies in the collective 'we,' not the individual 'I.'"[7] So yes, as a leader, you are a follower. All of us must follow directions and meet needs when at work and participate in the "one of many, together" aspect of working on a team. Building relationships and showing that you care about the work and the people help to enhance your leadership skills.

However, you bring more to the table. You are not just an employee who gets told what to do. You have a hand in forming and determining your role. *You* are the driver here, not your boss or your predecessor. You may find yourself meeting needs and taking orders, but at the same time, your role within the organization is a blank canvas. As you show interest and ability in certain areas, your position and your reputation will become more defined.

If you're in marketing and show a knack for writing copy, you will probably be asked to write more. If you're in sales and have an idea to move a product faster, you will probably be asked your opinion on other sales strategies. If you're in product development and show a deep understanding of what will meet the needs of your customers, you will increasingly be viewed as an employee who sees the big picture.

Knowing this, what can you do today to begin to shape your role at work into something that highlights your strengths and supports your interests? How can you take control of the way your colleagues and your employer view and utilize you?

How can you take initiative?

Chapter One Questions

Evaluate: In what ways do you see that your current organization may be "asleep at the wheel"? In what ways is it on the defensive? In what ways is it on the offensive? What is happening with the competition, regulation, innovation, and products in your industry? What are the emerging needs of your clients or customers? What topics are trending in social media or industry publications? Finally, how do your work and your role fit into this big picture? What can you do to add more value?

_____

_____

_____

_____

_____

_____

_____

_____

_____

_____

_____

_____

Evaluate: Think about the people with whom you interact at work. Who at your workplace models initiative, and how has it impacted his or her career? Who is the approver? The gatekeeper? The subject matter expert? The naysayer? Make some lists and then evaluate whom you need to get to know better, whom you need to placate, and whom you need to avoid. How will you branch out in practical ways to build these relationships?

_____

_____

_____

_____

_____

_____

_____

_____

_____

_____

_____

Evaluate: Look back over the past six months on the job. Have you been waiting passively to be noticed or recognized? Have you raised your hand to work on a new project team? Have you taken initiative in creating and crafting your workload, utilizing your strengths, and taking control of your present and future career? What is a first step you can take this week to take ownership of your career path?

_____

_____

_____

_____

_____

_____

_____

_____

_____

_____

Take Action: Work on developing a clear understanding of and explanation for "your brand." List out the strengths, ideas, and experiences you have to offer. One way to do this is to imagine what words or phrases you would want your colleagues and manager to say about you.

What are your short-term goals and long-term vision? (They don't have to be permanent or perfect; just a simple sentence about them will suffice.) How would you like to advance at your current workplace? To what work do you aspire?

Answer the questions above and assess. What action can you take in the next seven days to become the person you aspire to be? Taking one small action each day is enough.

Chapter One Notes

_____

_____

_____

_____

_____

_____

_____

_____

_____

_____

_____

_____

_____

_____

_____

_____

_____

_____

_____

_____

_____

_____

CHAPTER TWO

Define Boundaries

When you're driving and come up to an intersection with a red traffic light, you likely are law-abiding and stop. People have different approaches to what they do next. Do you stick around a few seconds after the light turns green, just to make sure that everything is clear? Do you hit the gas pedal right when the light turns green? Or do you begin to roll slowly forward as soon as you see the cross traffic stopping, even if the light is still red?

Red lights are boundaries we all heed, yet each of us moves around them in different ways. Some of us are more cautious; others are more daring. Some wait for permission to go. Others just go as soon as they feel that the way is clear.

There are red lights in the professional world, too. These boundaries are not to be crossed—or are they? As a point of reference, when I allude to the possibility of crossing boundaries, I refer to the context of roles, projects, or new initiatives. There are absolute legal and ethical boundaries in place that should never be crossed.

As you work to define your role, you will undoubtedly run into boundaries. Some of these will be self-imposed, perhaps by your own limited thinking. Others will be real and typically set from an external source, such as a budget, a regulation, or a contract. The way you handle moving around these boundaries will determine how your role and results will take shape.

In other words, as you take initiative, you'll have to navigate some red lights. The best way through these intersections is to be enterprising while also being aware of what's off limits.

Real Red Lights

While some red lights are imagined or self-imposed, most organizations do have real red lights that all employees are expected to abide by. It is fundamental to understand that each organization is different. One organization's boundary may be another's free-for-all. The way to understand the organization's culture and detect the boundaries is to be curious and observe the behavior of your colleagues.

To take initiative, you simply must spend more time doing your job. Create, deliver, produce, and focus on results while spending less time determining what's expected of you on a small-scale, case-by-case basis. It's time to figure out what boundaries do (and don't) exist at work. Without clear boundaries, you'll spend your time waiting for an invitation to do something that could easily have been done last week.

The best way to do this is to get to the point. Have a conversation with your boss, supervisor, or employer about what is expected of you and what the *real* boundaries are in your work culture and for your specific role. Taking initiative is essential, but you also don't want to cross a line or step out of the scope of your role. Ask your manager when the right time and place is for you to voice your input. Is there freedom for you to bring up concerns and ideas in meetings with other employees? What about in interacting with a client during a sales pitch or project? What is off limits? What are the hard edges or guard rails? Where is your discretion regarding budgets, client requests, process adjustments, or project management, to name a few? Don't be surprised if you get a response that begins with "I'm glad you asked that."

What you're going to find is that the hard edges are much further out than you ever would have thought. The absolute no's are few and far between. The lights that you perceive as red are many times yellow or green.

Defining the boundaries will help you to know where you are free to take initiative in a way that doesn't jeopardize your reputation or hinder your progress. Once you have defined the parameters of your role, you can do away with any unnecessary hesitation when it comes to voicing your input. Once you establish a record of delivering value, you can advance those boundaries further out to gain more responsibility.

Imaginary Red Lights

The next time you're in a business meeting, pay attention to how often you have concerns, ideas, or opinions that differ from the predominant view in the group. Then pay attention to how often you voice those concerns, ideas, or opinions. How is your point of view processed by the group?

One of the biggest self-imposed red lights in the workplace is the idea that you aren't allowed to speak up to ask a question about something you don't understand or to offer a different perspective on a proposed plan of action. So many workers are trapped by this, yet most companies *want* their employees to share more. They want employees to be engaged and part of the solution.

Instead, we tell ourselves that we aren't qualified enough to speak up. Or we believe that our ideas aren't valued. Or we assume that our bosses will want to do things their way regardless of what we say.

All of this may be true, depending on who your employer is and the organizational culture they have fostered. However, it doesn't mean that you should hold all your ideas and questions to yourself, and it certainly doesn't mean that your manager doesn't want to hear from you—he or she likely does! Now, it is important to acknowledge that in some organizational cultures, most innovative ideas are either outright denied or benignly ignored. If you find yourself working in an organization that seems like it is standing still, your focus should be on applying your good work within your scope of influence—within your own boundaries—and making your work shine.

Clarify your role, get rid of imaginary red lights, and speak up when the time is right. If you have an idea, share it. If you see a red flag, mention it. If you have a differing opinion, communicate it. Without this important step, your attempts at taking initiative will go nowhere, as it's impossible to shape your career when you aren't even willing to share your thoughts with others.

Bring Solutions

Part of speaking up means that you need to be willing to take action. Many employees who are bold enough to share their thoughts tend to focus on the negative. They are quick to talk about what's wrong or what's broken, yet they offer few solutions. When they do offer solutions, they are rarely willing to be part of those solutions.

One ground rule that I have used for team meetings is "no complaint without a suggestion." This approach allows people to point out what needs to be improved while also offering an idea. Consider framing your feedback that way.

When you make the bold decision to speak up, you will

quickly rise above your peers, especially if you also offer to implement the solutions you've come up with. This approach works as follows:

- Speak (speak up).
- Solve (suggest solutions).
- Act (follow through).

If you implement these steps every time you speak up, your voice will quickly become a welcome one within meetings.

Here are other options for exploratory questions to enlist others to work toward solutions:

- What could be another approach?
- Does anyone want to poke holes in this plan?
- What else is there to consider?

Navigate Red Lights

The actions, decisions, and solutions that have worked in the past to get you where you are—your success and accomplishments—will not take you where you want to go. Your employer likely already has set expectations of you, and that fact won't change unless *you* change it and up your game. You need to begin to make a new impression.

Part of this process is learning how to navigate red lights. It's time to stop hesitating. It's time to stop letting the idea of "I can't" get in the way of creating your position within the organization. It's time to understand where the real red lights exist so you can navigate confidently around them.

If you are adding value, delivering quality work, and providing support to your colleagues and projects, you're likely to find that your employer is much more flexible than you give them credit for.

Chapter Two Questions

Evaluate: List the absolute red lights within your organization (*not* your self-imposed ones). Talk to your supervisor to understand the real boundaries, as well as the freedom you have. (Note: If you have been delivering subpar work or have abused freedom in the past, you may need to prove yourself again before having this conversation.)

_____

_____

_____

_____

_____

_____

_____

_____

_____

_____

Evaluate: Think of a time in a meeting when you had a concern, idea, or opinion that differed from the predominant view in the group. Did you speak up or stay silent? What was the result? What can you learn from that experience?

_____

_____

_____

_____

_____

_____

_____

_____

_____

_____

Evaluate: What are some things that keep you from speaking up in a meeting or to a supervisor when you disagree with how things are being done or when you have an idea or a concern to share? List all the potential reasons you don't speak up, whether you feel that the reasons are justified or not. Evaluate if you should be contributing more or less frequently in meetings by asking your manager, teammates, and colleagues, "What would you like me to contribute to our conversations? How can I be more helpful in what I say and how I say it?"

Take Action: Take one area, starting small, and plan how you will *speak, solve,* and *act.* If you are nervous about doing this, try role playing the interaction with a trusted co-worker or friend. Think through the situation, challenge, or opportunity. Who are the stakeholders, and what is important to them? What are the benefits and risks to your idea? Anticipate objections and prepare thoughtful answers. Have your friend or co-worker evaluate your tone of voice, attitude, and content.

Chapter Two Notes

_____

_____

_____

_____

_____

_____

_____

_____

_____

_____

_____

_____

_____

_____

_____

_____

_____

_____

_____

_____

_____

_____

_____

CHAPTER THREE

Be an Influencer

At times, workers wait for their manager to navigate or determine their career path for them. They become complacent in the role or quit to pursue other opportunities, such as a new organization, a new role, or sometimes a new career path. These changes are often not made proactively but, rather, reactively. Navigating your career by reacting will not help you to move forward or develop into a leader. Emerging leaders have shared with me that they would rather move to a different company that is at the same level because they are afraid to push for growth and career development in their current role. This approach merely takes their mindset and habits to a new work environment and repeats the process over again.

Does this sound familiar? Have you jumped from job to job, wondering why nothing is working out? Or perhaps you've grown apathetic at work, waiting for something to change.

An organization is an intricate web of people and roles. Just like each strand of a spider web is imperative to keeping the web strong and firmly in place, each person and role within an organization is crucial to its overall success. Finding out how you fit in the web and how to navigate that space will help you to plan your individual growth and determine how you can become an influencer.

Passive Workers

Your role in the web has to do with what you can do and what you can provide. It has to do with your influence.

You probably wear different hats at work. You may have many responsibilities or be the "face" of a department. However, there is an invisible hierarchy that doesn't pay attention to job title or pay scale. It pays attention to influence. Knowing your role in that system is important.

When I consult with various organizations, I am able to assess a team quickly and determine its web or hierarchy. I can tell who is assertive. I can tell who is well-liked. I can tell who has influence, and I can tell who is passive.

You don't want to be passive.

The people who play the role of "passive worker" within the organization's hierarchy are stuck. They get assignments that don't interest them and assignments that are below their skill level. Because of this perception and, often, reality of inactivity, their drive to succeed diminishes. They become apathetic, and their existence in the organization is merely to accomplish tasks, regardless of relevancy or personal advancement.

You want to be an influencer. Influencers are the people who get stuff done. You develop influence by having credibility in your work. Do you deliver work that has quality and showcases your level of expertise? Influencers keep their word and their promises. Can your colleagues and clients depend on you? Another aspect of influence is what people perceive as your motivation. Do you have the best interests of the client, the team, and the work as your focus, or are you focused on yourself? Do you take time to reach out and offer help to others? How are you building connections and relationships on a personal level?

Take these actions and, slowly and surely, you'll build trust and influence among your teammates, colleagues, and clients.

Unless you are paying attention to the invisible hierarchy and working to become someone valuable and needed, you are at risk of becoming the passive worker.

Up, Down, and Across

There are two key ways you can gain influence: relationships and results. Relationship building with colleagues outside of your immediate team is key to building influence. These relationships are not built on superficial greetings in the office kitchenette or within the chatter on different channels on a digital collaboration platform. The relationship building here takes time and effort, using active listening and asking questions.

How can you add value to the interactions you have with other people? How can you add interpersonal value to work that may seem transactional on the surface? You can start by asking questions. You build rapport by being genuinely interested in your colleagues' work and what is important to them.

Some simple, work-based questions you can start with include:

- What projects are keeping you busy?

- What is interesting about the work you're doing?

- How can I help you or make this easier?

That last question serves two purposes because it can be used to build a relationship and shows willingness to be a collaborator and deliver quality work. Influencers consistently develop and nurture relationships and deliver quality work.

Assess the value that you are delivering to your team and to your internal customers. What else can you do to add value? If you are unsure, then ask them. (See the Stop, Start, Change, and Continue model in Chapter Seven for ideas on how to get feedback.) Get the feedback and then make the changes necessary to improve. It is this slow and steady development of relationships and refining of the work you do that builds your credibility and your influence.

Permission Versus Forgiveness

Passive people frequently need permission for little steps they take within their work. They need confirmation that teammates or managers approve of what they're doing. The approval of others is a safety net. It's a risk-free way of navigating around obstacles and insecurity. However, passive people rarely control their careers, their success, and their advancement.

If you're looking for a cliché sign that it's time to turn things around, this is it. You are the boss of you, and the only permission you need to move forward is your own. No one is going to hold your hand and usher you into a promotion. If you want to be an influencer in your role, you need to own your decisions, your career, and your future. Don't be afraid.

Much like bodybuilders only get stronger by lifting their maximum weight, you will only move forward by having the boldness to do what needs to be done when it needs to be done. It's not going to feel comfortable, but this isn't about comfort. It's about growing, changing, and becoming your best. Oftentimes this means moving forward with uncertainty.

There have been many times in my career when I've

needed to act. Instead of waiting and stalling and asking permission, I moved forward. I understood that if I waited for permission, the opportunity would be lost. The thing would never get done. So I acted. Sometimes I had to take the heat and ask for forgiveness.

Some time ago, I had an opportunity to develop a product for a client. The client's needs and my team's talents were aligned. We could build something that they desperately wanted. The situation as a whole supported the mission of my organization, so I knew that it reflected what my employers ultimately wanted: to serve in the client's best interest. However, my first obstacle was that we did not have a formal process for developing new products and services for our clients. Without a formal process, it would have taken me months to get a patchwork of meetings and documentation for buy-in from the senior leaders of each department that would need to be involved. I knew that if I waited for permission to create this product, then one of our competitors would fill the void in the market.

We had all the ingredients to make it happen, so I moved forward. Immediately, the weight of my decision was on me. I leveraged my relationships with subject matter experts from across the organization, and they agreed to work on the product in addition to doing their regular work. They knew that the product would help our clients. Basically, I had people working on the product under the radar. However, despite my discomfort, I was confident that I had made the right call.

Ultimately, I had to reveal what was going on and the daring decision I had made. I had to ask forgiveness for moving forward on my own (or "going rogue" as my Vice President called it), but I also had the data about what the clients wanted and a robust solution that had a very minimal cost to develop and maintain! The project had momentum that couldn't be held back or ignored. That rogue project was launched as a product, and three years later, it served as the foundation for an entirely new product and service portfolio.

My discomfort was a sign that I had pushed things to the edge. However, it was that very act of taking things to their limit that showed everyone, including myself, what I was capable of doing. When you make your decisions and push it to the edge, you, too, will find what you're able to do. And you just may impress yourself.

One final piece of advice here, especially when you may be in the throes of enthusiasm for your idea, is to weigh the risks and benefits before you jump into a new initiative, especially if you are going rogue. Make sure that you are delivering 100% on your projects before you take on anything else.

Assess the current limitations and boundaries you need to work within. What are the hard lines regarding ethics, roles and responsibilities, laws and regulations, company mission and values, and costs? From there, you can assess the playing field you have laid in front of you.

Develop Your Confidence

You may be reading this and nodding your head in agreement, thinking, "I need to take more risks. I need to find the edge. I need to ask for forgiveness, not permission. I need to take control."

One of the best things you can do to develop the confidence you need to take some of these steps is to find a mentor or career advisor who can help you to navigate those first big decisions you'll have to make on your own. This can be someone who is a veteran at your role or someone who is experienced in your industry. These experts make the best kinds of mentors because they know first-hand what you're facing. They can offer guidance and advice on what to do next, help you to identify big and little opportunities, and help to boost your confidence as you move from a passive employee to an active influencer. Join an industry or specialty interest group as well to gain information about trends and widen your professional network.

Another great resource is taking online classes from reputable organizations. LinkedIn Learning, masterclass.com, and udemy.com are all great places to start. These platforms will help you to supplement your knowledge about a variety of topics and sharpen your skills, maybe even learn new ones, which will translate into more confident decision-making.

Times Are Changing

Decades ago, employees could remain stagnant in a job and still be rewarded, but this is not the case anymore. Today's workforce is more competitive than ever, and the work environment is increasingly fast-paced and can feel as if it is changing non-stop. To move forward, you must be assertive. You can't be passive. You need to build relationships and establish and maintain a track record of delivering high-quality work that shows your value.

Awareness of your organization's hierarchy and invisible web of influence is one crucial element. The other is building your skills so that you have the confidence you need to make decisions and take control of your career.

Chapter Three Questions

Evaluate: Would you characterize yourself as a passive employee, fulfilling a narrow role defined by the organization, or as an influencer with valuable ideas that the leadership listens to? How would your supervisor and your co-workers describe you? How will you request that feedback from them?

_____

_____

_____

_____

_____

_____

_____

_____

_____

Evaluate: Is your natural tendency to be more cautious or daring, to ask for permission or for forgiveness? How does this tendency aid you in your career? How might it hold you back or cause you trouble? Describe a time when you were uncomfortable or uncertain because of taking a risk in your career. Did that risk pay off? If so, what can the situation teach you about bold, decisive action in the future? If the risk did not pay off, what do you think you could have done differently to enjoy more positive results? Look back to determine where you might have misstepped and where you made good decisions.

_____

_____

_____

_____

_____

_____

_____

_____

_____

_____

_____

Evaluate: Are you confident in what you have to offer? If not, why? List the skills and abilities that make you say, "I've got this!" and list the ones that make you say, "I need this." Seek out ways to develop yourself.

_____

_____

_____

_____

_____

_____

_____

_____

_____

_____

_____

Take Action: List some people who would be good mentors for you in your career. Choose one of them and plan a time to meet this week to discuss your career goals and what advice he or she may have for you. Using the resources for Chapter Three listed in Appendix A, research and list some possible training or online classes that would enhance your skill set and your confidence. Register for one of these opportunities.

Chapter Three Notes

CHAPTER FOUR

Steps for Growth

People who are unhealthy know that they need to eat right and move more. People who overspend know that they need to develop a budget and cut back. Athletes who get injured know that they need to go through rehab and training to make it back out on the field. In many areas of life, we *know* the way out of our problems. But doing that thing, actually taking that first step, often feels overwhelming.

So far, we've identified why your career isn't what you envisioned it would be, and we've even looked at some strategies to get a clearer view of your situation. What we have not talked about yet is how you can change your position at work. Positioning yourself for career growth is about being practical and putting yourself in the right mindset with the right goal.

Be Coachable

Your situation won't change if you're not willing to accept advice *and* put in the hard work needed to shift your mindset and attitude at work. If you want to advance your career and be more successful, become coachable.

Professionals who want to grow and develop take ownership of their results, good or bad, and they do not feel
the need to defend or rationalize their methods or approach. They're willing to learn. If they make a mistake,
they own up to it and readily accept constructive feedback. It's not about being right. It's about getting better.

Someone Who Is Coachable	Someone Who Is Not Coachable
Is not defensive when challenged or when his or her ideas are questioned.	Does not listen to ideas offered by others.
Welcomes feedback and ideas for improvement.	Staunchly defends his or her own ideas and approach.
Wants to learn new skills and/or seeks development (by reading industry publications or professional articles, attending classes and workshops, and volunteering for new assignments).	Does not engage in conversations about development and interprets suggestions to develop new skills as criticism.
Has a goal to work on.	Believes that asking for input is a sign of weakness and is uncomfortable acknowledging and discussing weaknesses.
Asks for help if needed.	
Takes ownership of his or her progress.	

Where do you fit? In your work situation, do you tend
to respond to correction or discipline with a coachable

attitude, or do you shut down or become defensive? People are not inherently coachable or uncoachable. We all have moments when we are either coachable or not. It's up to you to assess yourself in each situation and endeavor to become coachable for the sake of growth.

Coachability is important because it provides the proper mindset for learning the skills needed to advance in your position and career. The more skills you have, the more valuable you can become in the workplace.

Becoming Coachable

Three colleagues—Alan Fine, John Whitmore, and Graham Alexander—developed one of the most successful coaching models, the GROW Model.[8] The GROW Acronym represents the four core components of any decision-making process:

> **G:** The Goal the individual seeks to achieve
>
> **R:** The Realities a person should consider in the context of the decision process
>
> **O:** The Options open to the decision maker
>
> **W:** The "Will" or "Way Forward" as a specific action plan that maximizes the specialty and proactivity of the GROW Model.

The GROW model focuses on action, so it works best for getting practical things done. People around the world have used it to work on projects, form new habits, apply new skills, and improve performance. You can use this model to become more coachable or to reset your mind and attitude when it comes to work. You can coach yourself using the GROW model and use the questions to feel confident that you are considering different options and setting a path toward progress.

Let's walk through the model at a high level with an example.

- *Goal*: I want to achieve professional certification in my field by March 31.

- *Realities*: The certification will increase my credibility with clients and in my network. Study and preparation for the certification exams will take approximately 120–150 hours.

- *Options*: The timeline for studying will require focus and will consume free time, especially on weekends. There is a possibility that my organization has a development budget that can help to pay for a certification preparation class or even the fees for taking the exam.

- *Will or Way Forward*: My next step is to talk to colleagues who currently have the certification to ask for their perspectives. I also need to research exam preparation options (live or online classes and self-study).

To implement the GROW model, review the steps provided in the resources for Chapter Four in Appendix A.

Moving Forward

You can use this method to establish your goal. Your next step toward a better, brighter future involves tackling this goal and seeing it through. Here's where you're going to run into some adversity. Your goal may teeter on the edge of what you are comfortable with doing. However, one thing is true: you will never be the same.

This is the day you will begin to shed the former

hesitant or passive you and put on the new high-performance, highly valued version of yourself. This is when the evolution that's been happening on the inside begins to show on the outside. People are going to notice, and they're going to like what they see.

And so will you.

Chapter Four Questions

Evaluate: I often ask coaching clients to assess what motivates them professionally. Here is a partial list of options to consider:

Salary/Benefits	Level of Risk
Problem Solving	Creativity
Power	Reputation
Recognition	Security
Innovation	Growth
Flexibility	Control
Variety	Service
Independence	Belonging
Teamwork	Cooperation
Impact	Creativity
Steadiness	Accomplishment
Culture	Challenge
Boldness	Diversity
Accountability	Rewards

What motivates you in your job?

Now consider areas apart from work. What motivates you

to take action on what you know to be the right way forward? Think of your family, friends, hobbies, social activities, and lifestyle. Are your professional and personal motivators similar? How do they differ? Which ones can you adapt and leverage to help you develop in a new area?

_____

_____

_____

_____

_____

_____

_____

_____

_____

_____

Evaluate: Look at the list below of six positive qualities of a person who is coachable. How would you rate yourself on a scale of 1–5, with 1 being "totally not me" and 5 being "I do this consistently"? If your score is less than 20, consider what changes you need to make in your attitude or mindset. Ask a friend or co-worker to keep you accountable in your efforts to become a more coachable employee and give this person permission to be candid with you when he or she sees you exhibiting the behavior that you want to change.

Someone who is coachable:

- Is not defensive when challenged or when his or her ideas are questioned.
- Welcomes feedback and ideas for improvement.
- Wants to learn new skills and/or seeks development (by reading industry publications or professional articles, attending classes and workshops, and volunteering for new assignments).
- Has a goal to work on.
- Asks for help if needed.
- Takes ownership of his or her progress.

_____

_____

_____

_____

_____

_____

_____

_____

_____

_____

_____

Evaluate: Practice coachability by asking your manager or a fellow employee for honest feedback on a recent project you completed. Take notes on what he or she says. Ask for ideas on how you can improve. As much as possible, listen to this person's assessment objectively and dispassionately, seeking practical changes that you can make to do better in the future. Approach this process with the mindset that your manager and colleagues have your best interest in mind and support your professional development.

_____

_____

_____

_____

_____

_____

_____

_____

_____

_____

Take Action: Look at the goals you listed at the end of Chapter One. If necessary, add to or clarify them. Then choose one goal and take it through the questions and steps of the GROW model as described in Appendix A. Once you are confident in the direction you need to go, commit to seeing this goal through to completion.

Chapter Four Notes

_____

_____

_____

_____

_____

_____

_____

_____

_____

_____

_____

_____

_____

_____

_____

_____

_____

_____

_____

_____

_____

_____

_____

Part Two:
Your Role As a Manager

CHAPTER FIVE

Be a Great Manager

You've taken action. You've set goals and are moving toward completing them. You're developing your skills and evolving as a professional. You're becoming a stronger force within the workplace.

Before you know it, you're going to get promoted, be assigned a new project, or get put on a tactical team. You're going to hit that leadership role that seemed like a distant dream not too long ago. However, there's a catch. Becoming a manager is much more than a title change. It is a door into a completely new system or culture to which, yet again, you are expected to adapt. Much of this is because a manager is not an individual contributor. Managers are responsible for a positive work environment for several employees.

In the leadership workshops that I facilitate, one of my favorite activities is to compile a list from the participants of words or phrases that describe their best managers. Here are the attributes that appear most frequently:

- Adaptable
- Appreciative

- Available and approachable

- Calm

- Caring toward the employees and committed to helping them achieve career aspirations

- Giving constructive, active feedback

- Good at listening

- Efficient and organized

- Setting clear expectations and communicating direction

- Supportive.

Expected to Produce

In a corporate culture, it is now up to you, the manager, to ensure that your team is producing and not falling into the trap of becoming passive and indecisive—two of the biggest threats to anyone's career and an organization's overall success. Your organization may already have defined core values that dictate the expected culture, but this can also complicate things if your management style does not align with the desires of upper management.

You will need to make the organization's goals your goals and find a way to motivate your team to do the same. You'll have to connect the dots between the big vision cast by corporate and the day-to-day responsibilities of your group. A great manager must help to make the link between the work that is done and the measures of the success of the organization. What projects support the objectives and key results, and how can the team make an impact? What work is most important? This last question is simpler to ask than to answer.

On top of this, you are now expected to coach and

develop your team. You're expected to give feedback on past performance while also offering direction and help for future progress. Setting clear expectations is one of the most impactful tasks to give the team a solid foundation. Ultimately, you have to find a process that reflects the expectations being handed to you from your superiors while navigating the personal relationship you have with your team.

This can be overwhelming when you are an emerging or new manager who recently was responsible for no one but yourself. How do you excel? How do you hit the ground running and thrive in your role? It all comes down to adopting new skills, a new mindset, and a new systematic approach.

New Skills

There are two things that usually determine if employees are initially happy in their job: their paycheck and their manager. These are typically the first level of conditions for satisfactory employment. You may not be able to determine your team's pay, but you can determine the type of manager you will be.

A Flexible Approach

One of the most important behaviors needed of a manager is the ability to adapt and customize each situation to each individual. Every person operates differently, and in order to connect with the different behaviors and personalities, you must flex your approach.

Sometimes I get pushback from participants in workshops about that notion. They challenge it with "I do my best to be fair and treat everyone the same." While I agree that your staff should feel that they are treated with respect, they also don't want to be treated or communicated with exactly the same. That doesn't set people up to thrive.

Fair does not mean equal, and you need to vary your leadership and communication styles to the person in the situation based on his or her goals, project work, and experience, as well as your own personality and style. How are you individually managing each employee? Are you considering his or her:

- Communication preferences?

- Motivation?

- Career aspirations?

- Strengths, weaknesses, and blind spots?

- Skills and abilities?

- Experience in the role and with the organization?

When I began leading an existing team after the manager left the organization, I sent out a list of questions to my new staff members, asking them about their preferences and perspectives on themselves and the work:

- How's it going in the department? What's working well, and what isn't?

- How do you prefer to be recognized and rewarded?

- What is an aspiration you have for your role in the organization or your career?

- If you had a magic wand and could fix or improve one thing about your job, what would it be?

Consider this: An employee who is assigned to a new project will need more guidance at the start and along the way. An employee who is assigned something he or she has done numerous times will need much less of your time and attention. The idea is that by flexing your style to the person and the project, you can help your team in the ways they need it most.

A unique way of implementing this is to look at standard work hours versus a flex-schedule. Standard hours require team members to be in the office or online or available for meetings during set working hours. A flex-schedule allows more flexibility (hence the name). It gives employees some liberty as to when they show up and when they go home, as long as they work a full day—however your Employee Handbook and Human Resource Department define that—and are present during peak hours, the times when all employees are required to be present. Some organizations handle this by stating core working hours, perhaps 10 a.m. to 3 p.m. Some people want to work earlier hours in the day; some want to work late. By being flexible with your work hours, you can meet the needs and preferences of your employees and facilitate getting the work done.

As a manager, you can choose what is important based on your team, the work, and the organizational culture.

The Right Communication

It's common to think that as a manager, you always need to be accessible and continually engaged with your team and supportive of them. I've seen many new managers offer an open-door approach, only for it to lead to burnout as interruptions and distractions pile up.

Rather than allowing your team to come to you whenever and wherever, it's best to set some communication expectations. A "no email Friday" or some closed-door hours will allow you to be the approachable manager you need to be without compromising your own work time.[9] Conversely, you could have open-door hours during which your employees know that they have the liberty to come and meet with you.

Image Matters

Many first-time managers want to be just one of the team. They want to be in on all the jokes, the chatter in the rumor mill, and all the diversions from work they had before they were promoted. They forget that by carrying the title of manager, they are viewed differently by their team members, senior leadership, and human resources. Because of the responsibilities and expectations that come with managing people, it's important to master the skill of managing your image.

Here are some ways to manage your image:

- Praise people in public; criticize in private.

- Keep negative opinions about the company and other managers and leaders to yourself.

- Control your emotions, especially anger, in the workplace.

- Don't point out a problem without suggesting an idea for a next step or solution (this again, right?).

- Don't share confidential information. This could include information about budgets, salaries, raises, potential mergers or acquisitions, product launches, and other corporate decisions.

- Don't joke about any topic that could be considered inappropriate or crossing a line.

Additional Qualities

Your role as manager is to be responsive, balanced, and professional without going overboard in any of those categories. You want to be a good listener by asking good questions and making few statements. Trust your team to figure out solutions as you guide them in conversation.

If you've been promoted within a department, you undoubtedly know of pitfalls and problems that existed in your previous role. You will want to remedy these, showing that you support your team and that you understand the intricacies of their day-to-day workflow and responsibilities. You also want to create healthy competition. Offer rewards and recognition for a job well done. This should not only motivate people to achieve more individually, but also help them to strive to excel collectively.

Ultimately, you don't want to solve every problem for your team but, rather, let them present recommendations and strategies. You want to be there for them, but you don't want to be a crutch. You want to communicate your position while still being friendly and relatable.

Instead of solving a problem for someone or giving the answer, you can ask the following questions:

- I think you've got this. How can I help you figure this out? (Offer to be a sounding board for ideas.)

- What do you think would be your first step?

- What is in the way of success?

- What's most important to get right? What is not important?

Top Skills

Having the right skills is so important that Google spent a decade researching what makes a good manager.[10] According to Google, a good manager:

- Is a good coach.

- Empowers the team and does not micromanage.

- Creates an inclusive team environment, showing concern for success and well-being.

- Is productive and results-oriented.

- Is a good communicator who listens and shares information.

- Supports career development and discusses performance.

- Has a clear vision and strategy for the team.

- Has key technical skills to help advise the team.

- Collaborates across the organization.

- Is a strong decision maker.

This list is a great resource when it comes to developing the skills needed to manage your team effectively and to draw the right kind of attention from the right people, such as the organization's influencers or senior leaders.

New Mindset

It's your first few weeks as a manager, and your mind is spinning from taking in and processing new information and making decisions. There are so many things you want to accomplish, so many people you want to impress. It's tempting to jump into things aggressively and assertively—only to find out that you don't know what you don't know.

Your new role requires a new mindset. It's time to pretend like it's your very first day on the job. People are more likely to ask questions on their first day in a new job. They're more likely to keep an open mind and gather input from others. It's the best way to survive in a new job, and it's also the best way to survive a promotion.

Here are some questions to ask:

- How is this (task or decision) typically done here? What are the official and unofficial processes?

- What outputs or metrics are measured, and which ones are most important? Why?

- Who makes the big decisions about X project/issue/client?

- What information can I share with my team, and what should I keep confidential?

- What problem can I solve that would make the biggest impact?

This mentality also helps you to reframe your relationship with your peers and your role's relationship with corporate. By hitting reset, you can go back to the beginning. You may discover which corporate processes or mandates do and don't work, and you can move to fix them.

Be the Best Manager You Can Be

To be a great manager, you need to create a positive, fruitful environment for your employees. This may seem like a tall order if you've only recently been promoted, but I'm here to tell you that you have what it takes. You've already accelerated your career. You took something that was stuck and made it productive again.

For this reason, you're going to excel as a manager. You adapt. You flex. You aren't rattled by change. In the next chapter, we're going to continue to dive into your new role as a manager, unpacking what it takes to implement an entirely new management system.

WORKBOOK

Chapter Five Questions

Evaluate: As a manager (or in anticipation of a managerial role), consider how well you know the individuals on your team. In what ways can you exhibit flexibility as well as boundaries with individual personalities, skill sets, and needs?

_____

_____

_____

_____

_____

_____

_____

_____

_____

_____

Evaluate: What is your image, in terms of both appropriate clothing style and workplace conduct? Is there anything about your image that needs to be improved for you to become more professional?

_____

_____

_____

_____

_____

_____

_____

_____

_____

_____

Evaluate: Managers often think that they need to be constantly accessible, which may lead to burnout as unfinished work accumulates. How can you create boundaries and set communication expectations to help avoid this?

_____

_____

_____

_____

_____

_____

_____

_____

_____

_____

_____

Take Action: Consider the list of the top skills of a good manager. In what areas do you excel? What areas may still require some work? Make a list of your strengths and weaknesses as a manager and write down two or three practical ways to improve in the areas where you struggle.

Chapter Five Notes

CHAPTER SIX

An Innovative Management System

As a new manager who has developed new skills and a new mindset, as I discussed in the previous chapter, you may be able to implement a new system. Hopefully, as your scope of responsibility broadens, you will have the opportunity to innovate and implement new solutions and practices. Gone are the days of seeing a problem and feeling like you are not able to do anything about it. You can be a part of the answer!

People say no to new things too quickly. This truth is never more apparent than when you're in the role of manager and you're trying to enact change for your team. However, innovation is essential to growth. By raising your perspective to a higher level, looking at the bigger picture of the situation and the business, you can get more relevant information. You are looking at and making decisions about the forest, not just the trees. Focus on asking how you can contribute to results on the big goals.

It's easy to shoot down an idea. It's easy to ask, "Why?" or "Is this scalable?" People do ask these questions with the intent of finding the best solution, yes, but they also sometimes ask these questions in order to feel smart and capable (see my discussion of the naysayer in Chapter One). The hard part is fostering a process and an environment that encourage ideas and innovation, but the payoff is worth it. Innovation can make things more efficient. It can make things better and faster, with less waste or effort. It can improve products, increase revenue, and decrease costs.

New ideas need to be fostered, and it's your job as a manager to push through the naysayers and champion an environment of innovation. It's up to you to set the framework. The alternative is a team that lacks creativity, workers who dare not speak out, and a culture that doesn't challenge itself to become better.

Fostering Good Ideas

The number one misconception is that innovation is turning something on its head. That's not true. Innovation is change, however big or small that change may be. It doesn't need to be extravagant or groundbreaking. Innovation can be simple and done incrementally.

Another misconception is that innovation requires competition within teams. The problem with that mindset is that you end up with a group of people who only try to poke holes when they should be trying to work together to make an idea succeed. It's up to you, as manager, to foster an environment in which good ideas are welcome and nurtured, not shot down. Too many good ideas are killed in infancy. People find one thing wrong with an idea, and the whole thing gets nixed.

Ideas must be developed. They have to be tried and tweaked. If the team believes in the goal of an innovative idea, don't give up on it! Work at it until the goal is accomplished.

To foster an environment of innovation, you can try a

few strategies.

1. First, you can facilitate idea days. Team members spend the day working on developing and furthering solutions for the organization.

Here is one tool to consider. Think about your team or department and choose one potential area for innovation. Gather your team to answer these questions to identify an area to focus on.

- What would you like to accomplish?

- What business idea would you like to work on?

- What do you wish would happen in your job?

- What business relationship would you like to improve?

- What would you like to do better?

- What do you wish you had more time to do?

- What excites you in your work?

- What angers you in your work?

- What have you complained about?

- What changes would you like to introduce?

- What takes too long?

- What is too complicated?

- Where are the bottlenecks?

- What would you like to organize better?[11]

2. Second, you can do innovation exercises with your team. Present a problem and then work as a team to find ways to solve it.

The following approach, coined by Edward de Bono, is simple, but the results are a thorough exploration of an idea through six clear modes of thinking:[12]

- *White*: Information that is available. What are the facts?

- *Red*: Emotions and intuitive reactions or expressions of feelings.

- *Black*: Judgment and logic.

- *Yellow*: Positive view for opportunities and harmony.

- *Green*: Creativity and new boundaries.

- *Blue*: Thinking about thinking.

3. Third, you can require team members to present a recommended solution for every complaint. If a naysayer finds a hole in an idea, he or she has to present a recommended solution, alternative, or at least a first step. This way, team members aren't just criticizing ideas aimlessly; they're becoming part of making the ideas better.

I used this approach as a ground rule for a management team meeting that I facilitated. Anyone who complained without a recommendation during our two-day, off-site planning meeting had to wear a gaudy plastic crown to signify that the naysayer felt he or she was above the hard work of figuring things out. It was a hit and a lot of fun, and by the second day, people were refusing to take off the crown.

Naysayers have their role to play, but it should be done in a deliberate manner and in a way that works toward accomplishing a goal, rather than destroying innovative initiative.

Guard Rails

The beauty of this is that you don't have to be the creative one. All you need to do as a manager is foster the right environment to allow the creative minds to work and act. You can do this by providing guard rails and by asking the right questions to spur innovative thinking.

The right guard rails will keep the work focused, keep you on track, and prevent you from drifting into an area that won't help or could even be dangerous. Guard rails will help a team to stay in the zone of possibility, rather than spending time all over the road.

Some guard rails to consider are:

- *Budget constraints*: How much money is available to spend? Do we need additional tools or systems? Can we hire, or do we need to use current resources? Is there a desired return on investment?

- *Time constraints*: How many hours per day or week can be spent on this? Where will this time come from (other projects or overtime)? What is the deadline for a solution?

- *Scope*: What is the need for a solution? Do we need a quick fix, or do we need to revamp an entire process or product? Are we looking for a small adjustment or a big variation? What are the deliverables and features? What are the metrics to measure the result?

There are also guard rails for you, as a manager, to follow when it comes to forming and leading your innovation group.

1. One rule is that you will need a team with varied

viewpoints. Usually, this means pulling people who have different roles in the organization onto your innovation team. It means finding people who come from different backgrounds or who tend to look at problems in unique ways. This range of perspective will help to boost creativity and generate solutions.

Set up your communication channels immediately. Sure, the kick-off of an exciting new project or venture can be fun, but don't forget to set up your communication channels.

2. You also need to learn how to work with the naysayer. I've talked a bit about how the naysayer can add value to a project, and it's your job as manager to know how to tap into that. Some tips for this are:

- Before presenting an idea to the team, go to your naysayer and ask him or her to pick it apart. Then you can fix what's broken before sharing it with everyone.

- If your naysayer says that you are off track, listen. While it's tempting to want to silence someone who points out that you've veered from center, it's best to heed the warning. The naysayer is probably right, and the last thing you want is to spend precious time on something that doesn't contribute to the goal.

3. An important ground rule is to help people be comfortable with ambiguity. Workers like clear direction. They like deadlines and defined deliverables. However, when it comes to innovation, your team needs to move forward even when they don't have all the answers.

4. When it comes to communication, the best rule is that all questions are welcome. The salesperson can question the tech person about a tech issue. Marketing can push research and development (R&D). The idea is that everyone is on the same level, working together to achieve the same goal. There should not be a limit to their roles in a hierarchy on the team when they are creating and solving problems together. People are not limited to their areas of knowledge. All questions, thoughts, and concerns are welcome.

Asking the Right Questions

Emerging leaders may have some difficulty with shifting their mindset from being a subject matter expert in their specialty to leading a team of subject matter experts. This is often because when you are a subject matter expert, one of the most important drivers of success is having the right answers. Subsequently, your ability to shine as a subject matter expert often leads to being promoted to management. As a new manager, you quickly learn the necessity of asking the right questions versus having the right answers.

When I managed the external training department, we supported clients by offering workshops about our products, industry topics, and various "soft skills." We worked hard to make sure that we provided training that met the clients' needs. We determined their needs by asking questions. For example, if a client asked for customer service training, we knew that something was amiss, but it might not have been accurate to assume that the staff lacked customer service skills.

The client made assumptions about the problem (our customer service satisfaction numbers were down) and the solution (our staff needed better skills). We narrowed down the issue to the real cause of the decreased customer satisfaction by asking, "What is important for me to know about this?" Frequently, we uncovered that the reason for the lower numbers wasn't a skill issue, but an insufficient tool or lack of process. Had we gone ahead with the original request for customer service training, we would not have been helping to solve the real problem.

Using questions to uncover information and gain understanding is vital to guiding your team, advancing your career, and moving the organization forward. To spur innovative thinking, you must ask the right questions. Here are some ways to get started:

1. First, talk to people. Ask co-workers how things can be better at work. Ask your team about issues they see. Go to customers or clients and ask them to identify the problem areas. Once you get an idea of what is working and what isn't, you can determine the best approach for making improvements.

2. Second, think about growth. Consider your product or service. Who uses it? Who could use it? What industries need it that don't yet have it? How do your current clients use it? How satisfied are they? What feedback do they have? Asking these kinds of questions can help you to think about your organization as a whole and how to innovate new solutions and products that can generate more revenue.

3. Third, encourage team members to job shadow one another. Bringing in a new perspective may uncover opportunities for change or innovation. Having a tech person job shadow marketing, for example, could reveal opportunities for advancements in technology that could make the marketing job easier and more efficient. Shadowing also allows people to see the impact and connections, the "web," among different divisions, departments, and teams. Gaining a new perspective on the organization and its goals is often a bonus!

Problem-Solving Framework

Now that we've gone over the rules of innovation and

ideas to get creativity flowing, here is what the overall problem-solving process looks like. Of course, this is something that can be tailored to your team and your approach, but it's a great place to start.

1. *Define and analyze the problem or opportunity.*

    a. What is the ideal? What is the goal?

    b. What would you like to change?

    c. What is telling you that there is a problem or an opportunity?

2. *What is the desired future state?*

    a. Clearly outline the specifics of what the new state entails. What does it look and feel like? What pain is alleviated? How will you know that the problem is solved?

3. *Idea Generation*

    a. Use brainstorming or other idea creation activities to get imaginative and resourceful options out of your head and documented (see Appendix A for recommended resources).

    b. Take the ideas generated and expand them to uncover clear options for solutions or next steps.

4. *Evaluate and narrow down alternatives.*

    a. Rank and rate options by an established criterion.

    b. List the consequences for choosing or not choosing each idea.

5. *Make the final decision.*

    a. How will you decide: consensus, rank, or majority?

    b. What are plan A and plan B? Can they be combined?

For more in-depth information, please consult the resources listed for Chapter Six in Appendix A.

Productivity and Prioritizing

One of the first things you'll probably notice as you start to innovate is that purpose can quickly get lost. You may find yourself *reacting* to moments in front of you when you should be *controlling* the process.

Planning comes down to keeping a calendar, a list of projects, and a list of tasks for those projects. For the sake of clarity, a project is anything that requires more than two steps to accomplish.

Planning what you're going to do before you do it will:

1. Significantly enhance your effectiveness. Author and productivity expert David Allen says that people often react to the latest and the loudest.[13] Everything seems like an emergency in the moment—everything except the need for a plan. We let chaos rule under the guise of a fast-paced environment. Meanwhile, we live our lives, day in and day out, without accomplishing anything. We're busy fighting fires when we should be figuring out how to prevent the fires from happening in the first place. Having a plan in place can keep the chaos to a minimum and can also enable you to respond confidently when issues arise.

2. Help you to build confidence. As you pre-plan your work, you are going to make better decisions. Better decisions lead to better results. Better results boost your confidence because you're moving through your to-do list and hitting your goals.

3. Reduce your stress. Something simple, like making lists and calendars, reduces the mental activity needed to keep track of things. This reduces stress and helps with focus because you'll only end up doing the work that needs to be done.

Here's how to get started with organizing your to-do list and developing an efficient plan. Take a pen and paper and write down the following items:

- All of the thoughts in your head that are unresolved: business projects, errands, personal work, home projects, any recent "shower thoughts" that popped into your head while you were shampooing. David Allen calls this activity a mind sweep. Spend about ten minutes on this. Get all the "I ought to…" ideas out of your noggin and onto a piece of paper. By getting these ideas out of your head and onto paper, you are taking the first step to resolving them. If you don't get the ideas and thoughts out of your head, then they will just keep swirling around, taking up valuable attention and energy.

- All currently documented but unfinished projects (the ones that are missing more than two steps). If you are currently using your email inbox as your default to-do list, start there and note projects that are related to emails.

- All your current and needed (but not yet started) projects and the tasks related to them. You'll also have some random tasks that aren't subsets of projects, and that's fine. Determine your three most important work projects and top three personal projects.

Every morning (or evening, for the next day), before looking at anything else, take a few minutes and declare the top three things you want to accomplish. You'll likely choose these from your project or task list, or you may have to handle something new and important that has popped up.

As the day progresses, you will undoubtedly be hit by new things demanding your attention, such as an email from a colleague, a request from your boss, or an error discovered in a report. But instead of dropping everything to focus on those new needs, I want you to take a step back and assess the situation. Are the new tasks truly time-sensitive? Are they more important than the existing tasks you assigned yourself for the day, or can they go on the list to be dealt with another day?

This is how you start to take control of your time and stop being a slave to "emergencies." One of the foundational frameworks of productivity is the Eisenhower Box (or Matrix), named for former United States President Dwight Eisenhower, who advised that important matters are seldom urgent and the most urgent matters are seldom important. This matrix allows you to sort your tasks by urgency and importance:[14]

- *Urgent and important*: tasks you will do today or as soon as possible

- *Important, but not urgent*: tasks you will schedule to do

- *Urgent, but not important*: tasks you will delegate to someone else

- *Neither urgent nor important*: tasks that you will eliminate.

How would your tasks sort into the matrix?

In addition to planning your day, you should plan your week. While choosing three things to tackle per day will get you closer to your goals, it may take a while if those three things are always from different projects and don't build on one another day after day.

Planning your week means looking back at the past week and ahead to the next, and it covers both personal and professional parts of your life. The steps are:

- Complete a mind sweep. Add to-dos to your task list.

- Collect and review all your notes (paper or digital) and physical items, such as mail, handouts from meetings, and receipts. File items that need to be filed away physically or electronically. Add to-dos to your task list and appointments to your calendar.

- Get your email box cleaned up to zero unread messages. Your inbox is not the place where you manage or accomplish tasks. It is a tool for communication, nothing more, so empty it and enjoy that sparse landscape of an inbox for approximately five minutes before the next message lands!

- Look back at the previous week and congratulate yourself on what you have accomplished. Look at your calendar to see what the coming week holds, what deadlines need to be hit, and what you need to start preparing for.

- Then look at your project lists. Consider what your top three priorities for the week may be.

- Record your top three for the week. Add your most important tasks to your calendar as appointments. This planning allows you to prioritize the time you need to get the work done. Make your best estimate of the amount of time that the tasks will require.

- When it's time to choose your three daily tasks, refer to your task list and your weekly top three. Pick the activities that will make the biggest gains.

Additional Tips for Organizational Success

1. Tasks that go together can be done at once, so batch your work according to tasks that can be done at the same time. For example, if you have spreadsheet work to do, batch all of that type of work across your projects. Batch tasks like research, reading, writing, analytics, and creative tasks. This will save you time and mental energy. Consider your work preferences, too. I am an early bird, and I get the best results when I do my toughest analysis tasks in the morning. Night owls who feel like they aren't fully awake until lunchtime should set their simpler tasks for the morning hours.

2. Process your email three times a day at set times, not every time a message comes in! If you have an instant messaging app on your desktop for work conversations, mute it or display the busy status while you are doing your most important tasks.

3. Plan your work (your top three) and work your plan each day.

4. When you're working, disengage from anything that beeps, flashes, or draws you in. Shut down social media apps. Turn off all notifications on your desktop and mobile phone.

A New You

To be a great manager, you need a new system that includes tips and tricks to maximize efficiency and cultivate innovation. It is vitally important for you, as a new manager, to be open to new ideas and actively create an environment that fosters them. Innovation is necessary if you want to see growth, and it is your job to provide a framework for innovation. Keep your eyes on the bigger picture and ask yourself how you can help your organization to meet its major goals.

Support your team members and encourage them to express their creative solutions to improve the company. Communication, which can be a challenge, is key in this process. In the next chapter, we will discuss how a good manager can communicate effectively with his or her team.

WORKBOOK

Chapter Six Questions

Evaluate: Are you developing an environment of innovation? Do you need to create an innovation team or work with those on your current team to foster greater innovation? Do you need to add new viewpoints or backgrounds to your team, and if so, which ones?

_____

_____

_____

_____

_____

_____

_____

_____

_____

_____

Evaluate: How can you show that you are open to new ideas and encourage those on your team to share their ideas? How can you value cooperation over unhealthy competition? What behaviors do you encourage or discourage in your employees?

_____

_____

_____

_____

_____

_____

_____

_____

_____

_____

Take Action: Is your workplace chaotic and stressful or productive and planned? Are you reacting to or controlling events? Following the process in this chapter, make a task list based on all unfinished projects. Then follow the process outlined to plan your day and your week.

Take Action: Look at the list of recommended resources for Chapter Six in Appendix A and the organizational/time-management ideas from the chapter. Choose one that is pertinent to your workplace environment.

Begin reading about, studying, and implementing that strategy this week.

Chapter Six Notes

_____

_____

_____

_____

_____

_____

_____

_____

_____

_____

_____

_____

_____

_____

_____

_____

_____

_____

_____

_____

_____

_____

_____

_____

CHAPTER SEVEN

Communicate with Your Staff

We don't instantly click with all our colleagues, and it's not unusual to have had a manager we didn't feel connected to at best and hated at worst. We might have had a boss who micromanaged or barked out orders, one who didn't understand the work/life balance, or perhaps one who pushed to be seen as a "buddy." We might even have had a boss who didn't attempt to get to know more about our goals and interests. There is an upside to the bad boss. Each bad boss experience is an opportunity to learn and to adapt to an uncomfortable situation.

As a manager, you have the chance to get it right and communicate effectively with your team. There is a way to connect with staff without being too overbearing, too friendly, or too obsessed with the details and micromanaging. You simply need to follow through in three areas to communicate effectively with your staff: articulate needs, set expectations, and have tough conversations.

Articulate Needs

One reason why staff don't get along with or feel connected with their manager is because the staff members don't fully understand the greater needs that their roles or tasks fulfill. They view assignments as trivial busywork and rushed deadlines as punishment. In reality, each deliverable is part of a bigger picture that the team member likely knows nothing about. As manager, you can work around this by implementing a few tactics.

1. Clearly communicate the objectives of the work that needs to be done. This goes beyond simply stating goals and giving deadlines. Rather, you take the time to explain why the task is important and how it affects the organization as a whole or at least the next-level goal. If you find that you can't link the work to a larger impact, then you have every right to push back at your manager or leader regarding whether the task needs to be done or if it can be removed. As manager, you want to make sure that every task you give your team has meaning and purpose. If you find one that doesn't, dare to speak up.

2. Balance the benefit of supervision with the freedom of autonomy. In a quest to be cool, new managers tend to reject micromanagement completely in favor of giving their workers complete autonomy. The problem is that when you give autonomy without explaining the needs of the task or project, you end up with deliverables that miss the mark and don't meet your needs. Then, in an effort to correct this, many new managers swing the opposite direction and fully embrace micromanaging their employees. If you manage too closely, you're in danger of setting up apathy or resentment, which will stifle creativity and learning. However, if you are too loose with your approach, you risk the team wasting their time and effort while making their best guesses.

Therefore, it's critical for a manager to delineate the requirements of the outcome of the work. What criteria must be met? Does the work need to meet regulatory standards or brand guidelines? What level of quality and thoroughness is needed: a rough draft, a keenly edited final plan, or something in between? What should the data source be: an estimate from the team or verified numbers and information from a legitimate source?

The best approach is somewhere in the middle, balancing clear expectations with a hands-off but supportive approach. Throughout my years managing teams, I had opportunities to lead interns as well as very senior professionals. Finding the right approach for different people depends on their skills and experience and the kind of work they will be doing.

For the intern, I would provide background information about the work and explain how it linked to the bigger goals of the department. I would provide specific information about what the final work should include and what tools and resources were available, and I would set frequent check-ins.

In contrast, for experienced professionals, I would essentially delegate the work and show complete trust in their judgment and approach. I'd tell them to ask me any questions they had along the way before the deadline. While these examples are quite different, each person had the autonomy and direction that was appropriate.

Communicate your needs while letting your employee figure out how to fill those needs. Assess and set the requirements *before* you delegate or assign work.

3. Hold people accountable. When an employee is out of line or misses the mark, it's tempting to let it slide. After all, as a new manager, you want to foster a good relationship with your staff, and correcting them seems like it would do the opposite. You may not want to come off as unnecessarily authoritative, but holding your team accountable for their decisions and actions is crucial to setting the tone for the type of manager they can expect you to be.

4. Confront bad behavior immediately. Communicate your needs and expectations. Then hold your staff accountable, not swaying from the standard. If you do not do this, your staff will notice, and you will seem passive at best and cowardly at worst. By tolerating their actions, you are reinforcing their behavior and communicating that it's acceptable. This can devolve quickly and cause relational issues with your entire team, as others may see your refusal to confront a situation as preferential treatment or favoritism.

5. *Know where the line of transparency is.* You want to articulate the big picture and how your staff fit into the organization's goals, but you don't want to give them too much information that isn't relevant to their jobs. If impactful decisions are in flux and it's a stressful situation that is distracting your team, you can be honest with them and say, "I'll share what is confirmed news to the degree that I am able to." Only share what is appropriate. Share what they need to know to get the job done and feel invested in it and the organization. Avoid divulging negative information or anything that makes their work seem undervalued or unimportant.

Set Expectations

Effective managers set and communicate clear expectations at the beginning of any job, project, or role. They communicate expectations about people, tools, processes, timelines, autonomy, communication, results, and goals. Lack of setting expectations is the *number one* area that contributes to interpersonal issues on teams and with work deliverables.

Depending on the experience of the employee and his or her level of engagement, the conversation that sets expectations could be very explicit and specific, or it could simply be a few lines in an email. Knowing how much to communicate to each employee is your job as a manager, but my general rule is to communicate one step further with more specifics than you think you need to communicate. That way, there is little room for error.

Expectations 101

As a team, your number one goal is to consider the client (or the person that you serve), so ask yourself what needs to be done to make sure that happens. What is the best way to achieve that goal? Determine what you need and then backtrack from there, figuring out how each of your team members contributes to this experience.

Doing this will uncover your expectations for each of your team members. Expectations should be established for everything your team does: their work, their deliverables, and their methods. You need to set clear expectations for:

- The processes or methods
- The priority of the work
- How to communicate
- How to behave within the culture, team, and organization and with clients. (These are invisible rules that most people don't know exist until they cross them. They reflect the edges that every organization has.)

When it comes time to communicate your expectations, be sure to include the following three things.

1. First, you must communicate purpose. Explain why your team members are doing whatever it is you're asking them to do. Be sure to show them the bigger picture. Say something like, "This matters because...," and really fill in the details for them of how their role is contributing to a much bigger plan. This phrase is also a handy way to check your own understanding of why the work is being done and what is truly the most important element for success.

2. Second, you must provide key elements. Explain to your team members what you expect in terms of level of accuracy, level of data, deadlines, brand expectations, and so on. Let them know what the must-haves are and be up front about who will need to be involved. If you have a budget for them to spend, let them know, and be sure to get as much clearance as you can to allow them to have authority over the project.

If you know the process they will need to go through and the tools they need to use, explain or confirm that information. You need to be able to hand them whatever they need to get the job done and remove the obstacles in the way.

3. Third, you need to communicate the desired results or outcomes. Your team will be more likely to present you with a final report or product that is on brand and detailed and can be used with minimal editing or changes when you give them clear expectations of the result you want.

This isn't micromanaging. This is arming your people with what they need to be successful.

Expectations for Communication

Recently I conducted a workshop for managers, and each participant had to state the forms of communication they use, such as email, text, instant message, phone call, and face-to-face conversation. Not surprisingly, face-to-face communication was ranked as the best form of communication for discussions like performance feedback, coaching, and relationship building.

In my first "real job" after college, I was in an administrative support role, assisting multiple professionals. One of my managers did not set expectations well. I was given many responsibilities, but I was not told about priorities. I worked without clarity on which projects were the most important, so I did my best to juggle the tasks, spread my effort equally, and keep the plates spinning while paying attention to deadlines. This was my best attempt at prioritizing the work, and I thought that I was doing a good job of it.

Wrong.

My performance appraisal came, and I got low scores in the area of prioritization. Apparently, I was doing it wrong the entire time and not focusing on the most important tasks. I learned a valuable lesson. From that day forward, I always asked my boss for clarity on what was most important.

This is the problem with communication at work. A performance appraisal should have nothing in it that is a surprise to the employee. Yet, how often have we all been waylaid by a bit of feedback that we didn't even know was an issue? It happens all the time. I hear the stories in my workshops and from my coaching clients.

Changing the communication landscape is something you will need to tackle as a manager. One way to do that is to set clear expectations. Tell your employees:

- Which projects or areas you want updates on and what metrics are important

- How frequently you want them to provide those updates

- Methods of communication that you prefer and ones you don't.

If you don't want them texting you after 6 p.m., say so. If you want a weekly update on all their projects, set that expectation. In turn, ask them what they need from you in terms of communication.

As I advised earlier, be sure to set expectations one degree beyond what you think is obvious. You want to over-clarify. People aren't mind readers, and you don't want any surprises to come up on the day before a project is due or, worse, in an annual appraisal.

The Tough Conversations

Let's say you're thriving in your role. Your team is working hard, and everyone is responding well to your new direction. However, you notice that one team member is consistently late. This person comes into work looking exhausted, and his or her productivity has dipped. You know that you should say something, but you hesitate.

Tough conversations are, well, tough. They're awkward and can result in unpredictable emotions from everyone involved. Plus, if you've been promoted above your peers, it's even more difficult to be in a position of authority, where it is now your job to give feedback. How do you confront others about their behavior or attitude when, not too long ago, you were in the trenches with them?

Ignoring problems won't make them go away, and your relationship with your former co-workers is going to shift regardless. After all, you're now the one assigning them projects and giving them raises and feedback. It's time to shed the old mindset and accept the fact that things have changed. The friendship you had is not what it was, and that's okay.

Your focus should be on doing what needs to be done to become an excellent manager. A part of this process is the willingness to have tough conversations. The longer you put them off, the more awkward things will become, and there is almost no chance that the situation will miraculously solve itself.

In my workshops, attendees list these as their toughest conversations:

- Providing feedback on performance

- Delivering bad news that will disappoint, anger, or sadden people

- Confronting a different opinion or approach.

Giving Feedback

The feedback conversation is usually the most difficult. Whether it's confronting an employee for arriving late every morning or discussing a lack of enthusiasm or a dipping standard of performance, these conversations are unpredictable and awkward. However, there are a few ways you can lessen the blow.

1. Schedule consistent one-on-ones. Nothing screams "something is wrong" more than a one-on-one meeting request that comes out of nowhere. By scheduling monthly or biweekly one-on-one meetings with your team members, you have a natural space to address any difficult topics—and any positive topics as well.

2. Practice makes perfect. Don't feel goofy about practicing your points out loud before the meeting. It's important to phrase things in the right way, but focus on just a few key sentences. After you begin the discussion and get to the point, you'll have to improvise and make decisions about what to say as you are present in the conversation.

3. Talk through it; don't avoid it. Some believe that when it's time to critique or correct someone, you should sandwich the hard truth with a bit of praise. However, this method of praise-critique-praise only confuses people.

People can see the critique coming, but then they are left with a mixed message when the conversation quickly shifts back to praise. Instead of trying to sneak your critique in, be more open about it. You want people to grow and to accomplish something, so create an environment where constructive criticism is the focus.

When I was in my mid-thirties, I managed a team in which many of the members were much more experienced and older than I was. Instead of shying away from performance appraisals and critiques, I decided to acknowledge our different experience levels, and in two conversations, I sincerely recognized that the team member could have been the department's manager and done a wonderful job! I chose to give balanced feedback in the appraisal conversation.

4. Ask for feedback. Ask your team, your colleagues, and your manager for feedback about yourself and what you can do to improve. Ask them, "What should I do in the work I produce or the way I interact that would be better?" Ask this question frequently and you'll reap many benefits, including that the feedback conversations will feel less awkward and uncomfortable. You'll be regarded as willing to seek self-improvement. Hopefully, you'll also make modifications in your work or behavior based on your team's feedback.

5. Be mindful of whom you're talking to. Everyone responds and reacts differently to feedback. The key is to tailor your tone, words, and approach to the temperament and communication style of the person you're speaking with. Some people will need a firm hand and direct words. Others will need a soft, understanding tone as you approach them respectfully with feedback that comes from a place of support and positive intent.

6. Be generous with positive feedback. It's important to note that positive feedback should be given readily. If a team member is doing a great job, say so. Be specific.

Explain how his or her hard work is impacting you, the team, the client, and the organization. Assess the ratio of negative or corrective feedback to positive feedback. Which do you provide more of? Strive to have the majority of comments be positive.

7. Act quickly. You don't want too much time to pass before you give your feedback, but if the matter isn't a threat to the organization or the employee's job, you don't want to surprise the person with a meeting. If you want to talk with someone about how a presentation went, then ask if he or she has a few minutes to discuss it. By asking first and letting the person know what the topic will be, you are giving him or her the option to accept or to postpone if it is not a good time—for example, if he or she is having a really bad morning or is on a time crunch to get something out by the end of the day. If the team member asks to postpone, tell him or her that you will check in soon. Then make a point to follow up the next day or discuss the topic during your next one-on-one. You want to provide feedback as soon as possible after the incident.

8. Be specific. When you give the feedback, define the when and where of the situation. Say something like, "At yesterday's team meeting, when you presented your concerns…," then move on to address the behavior. Remember to give feedback only on the behavior you observed. Do not make assumptions about what might or might not have been going on.

For example, if your team member seemed unprepared for a presentation, it's best to critique only his or her mistakes. Say something like, "You were uncertain about two of the slides, and the cost calculations were incorrect." After you have stated the problem, then you should talk about the impact—something like "I felt uncomfortable because the senior team was there, and I was worried that it would cause them to question our work."

You don't need to insinuate that the team member was

unprepared or even a bit overconfident. Simply state the facts and then close by asking what can be done to ensure that the situation doesn't happen again and what you can do to support the person so that the data is presented accurately the next time.

9. Be fair. You don't know what you don't know, so you must be willing to recognize that there may be reasons or explanations for what's been going on. You must also be ready to accept feedback yourself about what you can do to help make things better.

Unfortunately, there are some managers who would rather lay people off or allow their employees to work themselves out of a job due to ongoing poor performance than give feedback. I have seen this happen in organizations that don't manage performance well. There's just something about sitting down with someone face to face and talking about his or her trouble areas that's intimidating and unappealing.

But here's the thing: feedback can be positive just as much as it can be negative. You can use feedback to correct bad behavior, but you can also use it to build someone up. You can use it to change what you don't want as well as encourage what you *do* want from your employees. Just as is true with other skills, the more you practice giving feedback, the easier it becomes.

Receiving Negative or Positive Feedback

It is characteristic of a great employee and manager to receive feedback gracefully and recognize it as an opportunity to change and become better. Too often, people brush feedback aside. They don't take it seriously. They view it as an attack, and they refuse even to think about it. However, in order to grow, you need to learn how to accept, digest, and learn from feedback.

- *The first step is to listen.* Be open to what is being said and be willing to look at yourself honestly.

- *Next, consider the source.* The person may be extremely credible or someone with a bad track record. This will help you to frame the feedback and determine whether to discard it or work on it.

- *You also want to thank the person.* Be gracious and thank the person for his or her insight. Don't justify, argue, or over-explain. Don't defend yourself. If the person is saying positive things, don't minimize your effort or contribution. Thank the person for being honest and let him or her know that you will be considering what he or she said.

- *Ask for additional input.* Ask those around you to provide insight on how you can improve the way you work and lead.

Delivering Bad News

When delivering bad news that will disappoint, anger, or sadden the person, it's also best to broach the topic as soon as you can. If you don't, the situation will fester, and you also run the risk of the organization's rumor mill getting ahold of the bad news before you've had a chance to deliver it.

In the case of bad news, for example, if someone doesn't get the raise he or she wanted or the promotion he or she expected, you should plan on a face-to-face meeting if possible, but at least a voice/phone call. It's tempting just to shoot off an email, either to get it over with or to avoid the awkwardness of a face-to-face conversation, but that would only hurt the person's feelings more because you wouldn't be treating him or her with the respect that the gravity of the situation warrants.

If the person shows sadness or anger, be sure to acknowledge the emotion, whatever it may be. You may want to say, "I understand that this news is disappointing/aggravating/surprising…." Allow the person the chance to explain how he or she feels. Then, even though you can't change the situation, talk with the person about next steps. This leaves him or her with a plan of action. Sometimes the person who is hearing bad news gets overwhelmed and falls silent. That's okay. Just let the person know that you are available to talk further after he or she has processed the news.

Too often, managers don't want to hurt feelings or squash all hope, so they choose to be vague when delivering bad news, rather than honest and up front. This is a disservice to the other person, who deserves to hear the information wholly and candidly. A vague conversation is open for interpretation, and an employee may come out with an incorrect view of the situation. Therefore, it's best to be straightforward, even when it's difficult.

Confronting Differences

There's nothing like someone who thinks that he or she has all the answers. You're sitting with your team, brainstorming ideas or solving problems, and inevitably this person speaks up and says, "No, no. We should do it this way."

People like this are confident, assured, and dismissive of others' ideas. They act like they have it all figured out. However, what may really be happening is that they're trying to "win" the meeting. Their goal isn't to elevate the discussion. Instead, they are trying to be the ones whose ideas get chosen. They're trying to be right, rather than elevating the conversation to find the best solution.

These workers are usually short-sighted. They want to win the battle, but their actions don't help to win the war. The goal for a team faced with a challenge is to agree on next steps while preserving or even enhancing team cohesion during the process. The team ought to be chasing after the goals of a completed project, a unified and productive team, and a happy client.

I was leading a team that managed client relationships, and we were constantly in conflict with various members of the sales team over who would be the main point of contact for the client. The lead role was inconsistent across clients and sales territories and varied from coast to coast and client manager to salesperson. Our team wanted to be the principal contact for the client after the sale and signed contract, but sales also wanted that role to keep their relationship with the client active for service upgrades and contract renewals.

Should the client contact the client manager or the salesperson? Did it matter what the client wanted to talk about? Externally, the confusion meant that our clients often didn't know whom they should go to with their questions or concerns. Internally, it impacted our processes for handling requests and overall client satisfaction. We had to figure out the roles and processes that best served the clients, asking what was in their best interest.

We had to have many challenging conversations to come to a solution, and I worked with the sales manager for months on a new approach. That's because people usually feel passionate about their position and may not change or back down after one meeting. However, we kept our focus on the best solution for the client. It turned out that what worked for us was a mix of reassigning territories and client accounts and creating a new client support model to adapt to client needs. We were aligned from the start to support the client in the best way.

Stop, Start, Change, and Continue Model

The Stop, Start, Change, and Continue (SSCC) model is an easy way to frame a conversation, develop a balanced perspective, and identify actionable steps to make improvements in communication, job performance, giving feedback, and more. It can be used to brainstorm possibilities and then narrow the field to viable alternatives for implementation.[15]

Once you've thought about your problem or situation, you can implement the model. The model consists of four phases with leading questions that can help you to zero in on how each one pertains to your situation or idea.

○ Stop

- What is not working?

- What wastes time or effort?

- What is an obstacle? What is hindering progress?

△ Change

- What should we tweak or update?

- What has experience taught us?

- What can we learn from a subject matter expert who does something similar well?

→ Start

- What would add benefit?

- What new skills would help?

- What new behaviors would help?

- What new tools or processes would help?

∿ Continue

- What works well that we want to preserve?

- What will it take to maintain?

To use this model when giving feedback to an employee, you will first *stop* and identify the main issue by asking the leading questions. Next, you will encourage *change* by suggesting a new, better path. You will *start* this change by adopting new behaviors, skills, experiences, or mindsets. You *continue* down the path of what is working well, fine-tuning as needed.

Employees rarely choose to be problematic. Often they are not aware that something is not happening as expected. In fact, they typically believe that their behavior or work output is effective because they haven't been told otherwise. As their manager, you need to provide feedback and explain what each person on your team needs to *stop*, *start*, or *change*. Additionally, reinforce feedback on what they need to *continue* because it is working well.

Your feedback is most effective when it comes from a place of sincerity and empathy. Having empathy means:

- Recognizing the emotion in another

- Taking another's perspective

- Staying out of judgment

- Communicating your connection to the other person.

In addition to having empathy, it's important to support

the employee in the way he or she needs to develop and improve.

Communication at Work

Being a great manager is more than achieving results and productivity. It's communicating and connecting with your team every day in clear, intentional ways. It's giving them the information, support, and tools they need to do their jobs, hit goals, correct problems, and grow as employees.

Too many managers think that to win respect they need to be either best friends with their employees or distant and demanding, but these are both too extreme and not effective in the long term. A relational approach with empathy and proper boundaries and expectations is the right recipe for connecting with your team. If you manage to follow through in the areas of articulating needs, setting expectations, and having tough conversations, you will be able to make meaningful connections with your team. It is a balance of head and heart.

THE NEXT LEVEL · 109

Chapter Seven Questions

Evaluate: When have you worked for a micromanager? When have you worked for a boss who made assumptions or assigned tasks without giving clear direction? How did each experience affect you?

As a manager, which one of these tendencies do you lean toward more? What are the circumstances (such as stress or high-pressure situations, your own lack of direction or information, or attempting to look and feel in control) that lead to your non-productive behaviors? How can you find a balance between giving your employees clear direction and supported independence?

_____

_____

_____

_____

_____

_____

_____

_____

_____

_____

_____

Evaluate: What is your default mode of communication at the office? What modes (such as face-to-face, phone call, instant message, or email) are you using to communicate information? Is this the most effective way to be understood by each of your employees? Do your employees know what you expect, and if not, what do *you* need to change so that you communicate those expectations clearly? Ask them what they would like you to *stop*, *change*, *start*, and *continue*.

_____

_____

_____

_____

_____

_____

_____

_____

_____

_____

Take Action: Set up regular times to give and receive face-to-face feedback from your employees. How will you prepare for these meetings so that you have something substantial to offer each person? How will you prepare yourself to be receptive and gracious in hearing their concerns?

Take Action: Role play a tough conversation, such as confronting an employee who is underperforming, giving bad news about a desired raise or promotion, or redirecting an employee who is not a team player. How might the conversation be different based on the other person's perspective? Try using the Stop, Start, Change, and Continue model. Practice demonstrating empathy while staying focused and firm. Additionally, look at the suggested reading in the resources for Chapter Seven in Appendix A to see if any of those books can be used to help your conversational skills as a manager.

Chapter Seven Notes

CHAPTER EIGHT

Coaching for the Future

A great manager recognizes and affirms his or her employees' unique skills and talents and encourages them to push out of their comfort zone. You can help them to meet their goals by coaching them for the future. The role of the manager is to be a guide. As manager, you will recognize the demands of leading your team *and* meeting business goals by your own work. You'll give a framework for the work to be done, and you'll set expectations and goals. Most importantly, you'll have an opportunity to be a coach. Some people use the terms *feedback* and *coaching* the same way, but for our purposes, I use *feedback* to refer to information about past performance, whereas *coaching* is forward- or future-focused.

Coaches want others to improve and excel. They're not as interested in business goals or chasing success as they are in developing talent. Coaching is about potential and performance. It's not about teaching or telling others what to do. It's about asking questions that bring out the best in others. Coaching will connect you with your employees, and you can't outsource it. You can't expect books or podcasts or classes to do the heavy lifting. It's up to you.

If you're still on the fence or worried about how much

time it will take, know that coaching and bettering your team will reduce turnover, increase revenue, and boost productivity. By helping your team to be their best, you'll end up looking great to your superiors. The good news is that the duration of coaching conversations isn't the important element; frequency matters more. Shorter, more frequent exchanges add up and are effective.

Great coaching implements listening, providing support, and encouraging challenge. *Listening* means hearing your team members out and striving to understand their points of view. *Support* means having their backs and getting them the resources they need to be successful. *Challenge* means encouraging them to hit their goals, to take that step forward, to try something new that may require stepping out of their comfort zone.

Coaching is a delicate relationship that must be balanced by each party doing his or her part.

1. The role of the coach: You don't need to know the ins and outs of every job in order to give good feedback, nor do you have to be an expert in a field to provide guidance and help. Rather, encourage employees to establish goals, set a structure and framework to support those goals, and provide accountability. Along the way, you can help employees to identify problems or obstacles and even help to remove or mitigate them. As a coach-manager, you can connect with your employees by helping them to move forward in their careers.

2. The role of the employee: You can't coach someone who doesn't want your help. Therefore, it's important to find the right people for your team. They must be motivated to change and improve. They must be open to feedback and not get defensive when challenged. They should be goal-oriented and willing to ask for help. Finally, they need to take ownership of their progress. You are there to guide, direct, and provide structure and accountability. You cannot do the work for them.

The Coaching Process

The coaching process can be broken down into these steps:

- Clarify goals and the approach. Ask, "How do we want to work together?"

- Talk it out. Meet frequently in short bursts to get a compound effect. As a coach, listen actively and ask questions. Help the employee to refine his or her goals or work toward solving a problem. (One option here is to use the GROW model we discussed in Chapter Four.)

- Create an action plan. Have the employee come up with an action plan for how he or she will achieve a goal or solve a problem. Help to refine the plan, then ask the employee what he or she will commit to doing.

- Act. Between meetings, the employee should work toward carrying out his or her plan.

- Celebrate. Take time to acknowledge and praise achievement. Giving recognition is often overlooked in our go-go culture, but it is important for keeping up momentum and motivation. When people feel stuck, looking back at the progress already made can help to spur them forward. Celebrate the wins.

With success will also come some hurdles and setbacks. Here are some of the top challenges that coaches face.

1. Over-managing: It's important not to take over when employees get stuck or stall. Hold back from having too heavy of a hand or offering too much advice and overloading them. Focus on the positives and progress and don't worry about solving all of their problems. Help them to consider the options without telling them what to do.

2. Fear: The people you're coaching may be afraid of failing, so they may pick simple goals or easy targets that are low-risk and conquerable. You need to be ready for this and be willing to push them beyond their comfort zone. Push them to want to do more. You do this by: (1) acknowledging how they have an accomplished track record and (2) asking them how they can take just one next action to move forward.

3. Giving up: Progress can come to a screeching halt when employees stop being direct about their progress. They may say that they are overwhelmed or confused and they simply don't know what to do next. This may be an attempt to avoid the possible uncomfortable feelings, to change the goal, or to back out of the coaching situation. Often they *do* know what to do next; they just don't want to do it. It's your job to help them through this.

When I was 26, I was named interim manager at my company and had a chance for a formal promotion into the role. I remember feeling so unsure of myself when human resources scheduled the interview. Fortunately, I had a secret weapon. His name was George. He was an early mentor of mine and knew from experience that being good at what you do isn't enough to get you where you want to go.

I'll never forget his advice to me a few days before my interview. He said, "Take initiative with human resources. Go in there and tell them what you'll do when they promote you to manager. They want to know if you can lead. Leaders make plans. Give them one."

George later became my manager. Whenever we met, he asked me about problems I was facing or about what progress I was making toward my goals. He then asked me questions to help me understand how I could fix the problems or hit the goals.

Then he endorsed an action that I had brought to the table. From there, he had me talk about what my first step would be, and the rest is history. He coached me into progress, and all it took was a few minutes of his time twice a month.

Non-Verbal Communication

Whether you are coaching, giving feedback, or setting expectations, be aware of nonverbal communication. Crossed arms, leaning away from you, feet that are turned away from you, and lack of eye contact can be signs that someone feels uncomfortable with you or the discussion. Noticing this can allow you to work on connecting with those people in a better, more genuine way.

On the other hand, your own body language may give away any repressed worry, fear, anxiety, or stress you may have in any given situation. Be aware of how you're sitting, how you're positioned, and how your body language is communicating with those around you. Do not multitask when communicating with another person—no cell phone, no hands on the keyboard, no glancing at your screen to see what message has popped up.

In one-on-one meetings, try not to sit across from people. This communicates that you are an adversary, physically on the other side of them. Rather, try to make it so that both parties sit at the corner of the table in a 90-degree formation. Have you ever considered a walking meeting? It's just what it sounds like: having a meeting or conversation while taking a walk. This is a great method for communication because you're literally side by side and moving in the same direction. Maybe even grab a coffee while getting some fresh air.

Coaching Employees to Success

It is vitally important for a manager to coach employees to better habits and sharpened talents. Coaching your team members is a worthwhile investment of your time. As a coach, you listen, provide support, and encourage your employees to challenge themselves and step out of their comfort zone.

The coaching process includes helping the employees you are coaching to set goals, providing structure and support for them to meet those goals, and holding them accountable. As a coach-manager, you will provide guidance and help along the way, coming alongside employees and guiding them as they advance in their careers, coaching them to success.

WORKBOOK

Chapter Eight Questions

Evaluate: Have you ever experienced being coached by a manager? How did the manager equip you to meet your goals? Did you experience growth as a result of being coached?

Are you currently coaching one or several of your employees? How can you make time in your busy schedule to coach someone?

_____

_____

_____

_____

_____

_____

_____

_____

Evaluate: What is the difference between coaching and telling people what to do? How can you be more effective as a coach, affirming your employees and pushing them out of their comfort zone? How can you help employees to reach their goals, perhaps using the GROW model?

_____

_____

_____

_____

_____

_____

_____

_____

_____

_____

Take Action: Look at your team with the mindset of a coach. What untapped potential and talent do you see in each employee? Who needs guidance? Who needs to be challenged more? Who needs accountability to keep working toward his or her goals? Write out your coaching vision for each of your employees. Use your face-to-face feedback meetings to talk to your employees about their goals and to work together to form an action plan for achieving them. Refer to the resource for Chapter Eight in Appendix A and use the question list to implement coaching in your meetings.

Chapter Eight Notes

_____

_____

_____

_____

_____

_____

_____

_____

_____

_____

_____

_____

_____

_____

_____

_____

_____

_____

_____

_____

_____

_____

_____

CHAPTER NINE

Effective Meetings

"That meeting could have been an email."

We've all heard or said this too many times. Maybe you even have a coffee mug with that statement printed on it. This complaint is so common because meetings are broken. They're too long and disorganized, and they involve too many people. They're easy to schedule yet difficult to do right. One poll shows that 46% of Americans would rather do almost any "unpleasant activity" than endure a business meeting.[16]

Many of us have a schedule full of meetings that waste time and don't produce results. And they're expensive. I heard of one organization that has a "meeting cost counter" on a wall in the conference room. Every minute, the cost of everyone's time appears on the counter. If you are interested in tallying up the total for one of your meetings, you can find calculators online or can refer to the resources for Chapter Nine in Appendix A.

The fact is that good meetings don't just happen. Good meetings are carefully planned and managed. They involve the right people gathering at the right time for the appropriate amount of time. People do see the value of meetings to help set and plan goals, problem solve, and define paths for results, and the majority (97%) of people consider it essential to collaborate to do their best work.[17]

A History of Bad Meetings

Some of the best meetings are the ones that are client-facing. Decisions are made, confusion is cleared up, and both teams end up leaving the meeting feeling better about their working relationship. Meetings with clients, in my experience, often have a higher level of accountability than internal-only meetings. Why is it that the same companies that excel at client meetings can't seem to hold proper internal meetings?

A meeting should take place only when absolutely necessary. But that's the problem. We're so accustomed to attending meetings that we don't know how to get work done without them, and we end up with too many unnecessary meetings on the calendar. In many organizations, it is an automatic response to schedule a meeting when there is a question, a need for additional information, a decision to be made, or a problem to be solved. Those may be valid reasons to have a meeting, but what is lacking is the definition of the *desired outcome* and the other elements of preparation that set a meeting up for success.

Bad meetings are typically formed out of lack of clarity about the work or project or by habit. Often the lack of clarity comes from unclear roles, processes, methods, or communication about the work. The habit part, well, that applies to continuing to meet just because you have done so in the past. Be honest with yourself about both the value you get and the value you give in any meeting. What are you willing to change about your meetings so they are more effective?

Best Practices for Meetings

Meetings should last only long enough to meet the purpose and objectives. But what we typically get in the workplace are long, unproductive meetings in which too many people weigh in (therefore, no decisions are made) while others wonder why they were invited in the first place.

Thankfully, there are some best practices that will help you to host quality meetings in your role as manager.

1. Determine the meeting's purpose. All meetings should have a clearly defined purpose that is communicated with the attendees. Purpose helps to keep conversation on track because everyone is pushing toward achieving the goal.

Here are the most common purposes for meetings and the corresponding outcomes:

- *Share and update → Information to impact a future decision.* This is the criterion you should use for any meeting that provides updates. Does this information impact a future decision of the meeting attendees? If not, then send an update via an email, status report, or other mode and make the meeting objective a Question and Answer forum.

- *Solve a problem → A solution.* Prepare a structured agenda that includes a problem-solving model or steps, such as:

  o Define the Problem

  o Determine the Root Cause(s) of the Problem

  o Develop Alternative Solutions

  o Select a Solution

  o Implement the Solution (post-meeting)

- *Make a decision* → *A decision.* Agree ahead of time on the decision-making process. Will it be by majority vote, by seniority or title, by level of expertise, or other criteria? In order to save time in the meeting, send background information as pre-meeting reading and ask attendees to come prepared for the discussion.

2. Carefully form the invite list. The important thing is to have only the right people in the room. Who is necessary to achieve the meeting's goal? Who has a direct stake in the discussion? What are their roles in the meeting (e.g. decision maker, subject matter expert, reviewer, approver, stakeholder)? Invite these people and no one else. Invite only the "need to have" and not the "nice to have" attendees.

3. Structure the agenda. Consider the agenda your road map to get to the desired outcome of the meeting. An agenda will keep you on track. Organize the agenda in the order of importance and give each topic a dedicated amount of time. When you have a colleague who starts to go off on a tangent, you can use the agenda as the way to reel the person in: "Are we on track here?" If attendees do want to spend time on the tangent or new topic, then have a quick discussion of the implications and determine if the new topic is more important than the planned agenda topic. An agenda should be a guideline, but it should also be flexible to adjust to urgent matters.

4. Determine how much time will be needed. Too many meetings default to hour-long blocks of time. However, a well-organized meeting can usually accomplish a lot in shorter amounts of time. Reduce your typical meeting duration from sixty minutes to forty-five minutes. Could you accomplish the agenda of your usual thirty-minute meeting in twenty minutes?

5. Assign responsibilities. There are three necessary responsibilities that need to be filled for every meeting. These responsibilities can rotate among team members as appropriate. Be sure to assign them beforehand so that people can come prepared.

- *Meeting facilitator*: This person is in charge of driving toward the meeting's goal. At the start of a meeting, the facilitator should restate the meeting's purpose and the roles of the various attendees. Throughout the meeting, this person should make sure that the conversation stays on topic and is moving forward. The facilitator restates decisions, clarifies information, and asks pertinent questions.

- *Timekeeper*: This person ensures that a meeting begins and ends on time. (The facilitator can also be the timekeeper if necessary.)

- *Note taker*: This person takes note of decisions made and action items, including who is doing what and when. Meeting notes should be emailed to participants and/or posted in a digital repository (e.g. shared or cloud drive).

5. Set ground rules. These can vary from meeting to meeting, depending on your needs and goals, but typically they should be a set of expectations for conduct. The ground rules should clarify how information and ideas are presented (e.g. one person speaking at a time, no multitasking, confidentiality) and how the decisions will be made.

6. Additional tips: If the purpose of a meeting is to

make a decision, then that meeting should be held in the morning when minds are fresh, not fatigued.

Make sure that the technology is running smoothly before the meeting starts. If you're a whiteboard user like I am, consider bringing your own markers because there are so many dried-out ones in the typical meeting room. (How does that happen?) Also, blue and black are the easiest colors to read. Avoid using red, yellow, and purple markers except to highlight or bullet.

If conference calls frequently occur with participants in different time zones, then they should take turns with who must attend the meeting at an inconvenient time. For example, conference calls among the Los Angeles, London, and Mumbai teams should alternate times so that the burden for calls late at night or very early in the morning is not always on the same time zone.

A great type of meeting to have during lunch hour is the personal development meeting. These "lunch and learn" meetings are when the organization brings in a speaker or showcases an internal subject matter expert or executive and attendees can learn something new over the lunch hour.

One-on-one meetings pose unique challenges and need some regularity to ensure a balance between the autonomy of the employee and micromanaging. These meetings should be very consistent in their scheduling, and they ought to have a balanced agenda, but the focus should remain on the employee.

There are two exceptions to the rule that meetings should not take place just to share information. First, there's the ten-minute stand-up meeting at the start of the day to get everyone on the same page about the status of the project or client so that the team can make better decisions about their work. The other exception is the "all-hands meeting" when all of the staff come together and senior   leaders   answer   questions   and/or   make announcements. However, these gatherings also need to be planned and kept on track.

Best Practices for Online Meetings

Although necessary for remote or dispersed teams and convenient for clients, online meetings are much more difficult to run well than in-person ones. While you still want to implement the standard best practices, you should also add the following to your to-do list for conference calls or online meetings.

1. Manage the meeting like a traffic cop at an intersection. The facilitator always needs to be calling the shots and directing the traffic. Do this by providing more structure than normal. For example, call out the agenda items as you move through them and offer frequent recaps of progress or decisions made. This may look like: "Okay, now we are talking about Agenda Item #2—Budget," then "We just wrapped up the decision about the budget, and now we are going to talk about the new regulatory rule."

2. Ask that people announce themselves every time they talk. If the speaker states his or her name, you will eliminate all confusion over trying to identify people simply by their voices.

3. Keep the agenda and notes visible on a shared screen (if possible). This helps people to stay oriented to what you are talking about.

4. Keep track of who has spoken. Check off names as each person speaks on a topic. If someone has not spoken on a topic, you can then call on that person. You can even organize the talking by simply calling on people in order and asking for their input. This keeps people from talking over each other.

5. Use the features of your online platform. There are various tools you can use for your online meetings, depending on your platform: virtual hand raising, chat boxes, emoticons, whiteboards, polling, and screensharing, for example. Take twenty minutes to dive a little deeper into the functionality you have available and try it out in your next meeting.

Best Practices for Hybrid Meetings

Hybrid meetings in which some people are face to face while others are calling in from remote locations are likely to become more and more prevalent as work cultures shift and more people work remotely. The following are best practices to keep in mind for hybrid meetings.

1. Treat it like it is an online-only meeting. Participants who have called in usually have trouble keeping up with the discussion in this type of meeting because the conversation is often dominated by those attendees who are in a room together. By treating the meeting like an online meeting, you're sure to include everyone.

2. Keep noise in the face-to-face meeting room to a minimum. Do not drag the conference phone across the desk, eat potato chips, have side conversations, or rustle papers. It's hard enough for the callers to hear. You don't want to exacerbate the problem.

3. Consider making it a virtual meeting only. As the logistics of a hybrid meeting get more complicated with more attendees, you could easily move the meeting to one in which all participants call in, even if it's from their desks. That way, everyone is on the same platform.

The Master of Meetings

At first, running meetings may seem intimidating. Calling the shots, keeping everyone on track, and pushing toward resolutions is not always the most comfortable of positions to be in when you're new to a management role.

But as you fight for shorter, more effective meetings, you will soon be the favored facilitator in the organization.

WORKBOOK

Chapter Nine Questions

Evaluate: What do you hate most about meetings? What regularly scheduled meetings do you find boring or a waste of time? Now describe a meeting that you have attended that was run effectively and concisely and proved a valuable use of everyone's time. What made it a successful meeting?

_____

_____

_____

_____

_____

_____

_____

_____

_____

Evaluate: Do you make use of online or hybrid meetings? Which of the suggestions shared in this chapter could make your virtual meetings smoother and more effective?

_____

_____

_____

_____

_____

_____

_____

_____

_____

_____

Evaluate: Who or what tends to sabotage your meetings, getting things off track and causing distraction and delay? What steps can you take beforehand to plan and prepare a meeting that will stay on track? If there is an individual who is derailing your meetings, how might a private, face-to-face talk with that person ahead of time help?

_____

_____

_____

_____

_____

_____

_____

_____

_____

_____

_____

Take Action: Using the resources for Chapter Nine in Appendix A, write out an agenda for your next team meeting and your next one-on-one meeting. What information needs to be given out ahead of each meeting? What is your purpose or goal, and how do you hope to achieve it through the meeting? After conducting those meetings, evaluate whether using the tool helped the effectiveness of your meetings. Tweak as necessary and continue to use a planning strategy to keep your meetings productive and efficient.

Chapter Nine Notes

_____

_____

_____

_____

_____

_____

_____

_____

_____

_____

_____

_____

_____

_____

_____

_____

_____

_____

_____

_____

_____

_____

CHAPTER TEN

Money Speaks

My friend Jonathan Sparling has a background working in college planning and financial education. He is an MBA and an Accredited Financial Counselor (AFC®). He's helped to develop a money skills program, and in this chapter, he is providing his most useful advice and tips.

Your career may take twists and turns, and you may find yourself in different roles or different industries, but the one constant is money. Sure, you want success, accolades, respect, and achievement, but you also want your hard work to pay off. Your compensation (salary plus benefits) is a consistent measure of tangible rewards.

Therefore, knowing how to make good money decisions is an important part of your career growth. Too many professionals grow in their careers without knowing much about investing, saving, and budgeting. They wonder why they're making six figures yet carrying so much debt month after month. During your time of professional growth and development in your career, you also need to learn the fundamentals of money management.

Professionals are excited to begin their careers and start that first job, but little attention is given to the financials behind most entry-level offers. These young workers fail to negotiate a better package, so they start their careers at a disadvantage—without even knowing it. They say "yes" to a job that can cover only a portion of their expenses. And instead of downscaling, many *add* to their financial commitments once that first job is secure. For instance, they take on car payments or have to start paying off student loan debt.

The fact is that most employers are willing to negotiate on salary and benefits, but few new hires request this. Rather, they start their careers in a hole and then spend upwards of a decade trying to dig themselves out of it, waiting for raises or promotions to level things out. Established professionals often make the same errors, slowly building their debt and spending as their income increases.

As they play catch-up to cover the day-to-day expenses, putting away for retirement savings gets put on the back burner. After all, if there aren't funds to pay for student loans, how can there be funds to pay for retirement? Crucial years are missed. Retirement plans go without any major contributions, and the magic of compound interest becomes less impactful with every year that passes.

All workers need to be money-smart as they enter the workforce and even smarter as they move through it.

The Importance of Negotiation

Making the decision to negotiate your salary and benefits package will only help your bank account and sharpen your skills. Failing to negotiate from the inception will result in missed opportunities. For example, if you stay in your first professional position for two to three years, you will miss out on thousands of dollars that could have been yours. You will also miss out on the experience of negotiation. When you move to your next job or promotion within the same organization, you won't have past experience to draw upon. You'll be starting from scratch as opposed to sharpening a skill.

To negotiate your salary, keep these best practices in mind:

- *Research the job and pay.* Get a baseline understanding of what your salary should be based on industry, experience level, and location. If you can get some numbers to back up your negotiations, you'll have automatic credibility. I have included more information about this in Appendix A.

- *Think about alternatives.* If a salary increase isn't doable, think about asking for other benefits, such as student loan repayment assistance, more vacation time, or contributions toward advanced education or training certifications and accreditations.

- *Practice having the conversation.* You'll feel more confident and be able to express your desires better if you practice having the conversation with a friend or family member.

Another factor of negotiating that many people don't consider when they're early in their career is the employer's offer to match retirement contributions. Not taking advantage of that match is leaving money on the table, yet most young workers say "no" to retirement contributions. As you figure your budget and negotiations, aim to maximize your retirement contributions and receive as many match dollars as possible (if you are lucky enough to have that as an employee benefit at your organization).

Flexible spending accounts are another perk that many employers offer. These accounts allow you to put money away and not be taxed on it. This is a great way to save for emergency needs and lower your taxable income at the same time.

Regardless of what the offer is, once you take out taxes, insurance, and a little for retirement, you are likely to net about 75% of your gross income. If their entry-level offer is $30,000, that will leave you with $22,500 to work with for the year. This number can impact your ability to relocate or secure housing close to your new job. Therefore, consider how much your take-home amount will be as you negotiate.

Best Practices for Financial Success

Overall, if you take your salary out of the equation, smart money choices don't have to be complicated. In addition to the tips from University of Chicago professor Harold Pollack, which you can find in the resources for Chapter Ten in Appendix A, I recommend that you:

- *Make sure that you are building an emergency fund first.* Build up a pot of $500–$1000 and set it aside. Only access it for true emergencies. This will give you a safety net as you invest or save dollars for other things. What constitutes an emergency? Well, it's not a last-minute vacation deal. Think instead of unexpected car repairs or medical bills.

- *Set realistic goals.* Have goals that you chase with your dollars. These can be immediate (goals you plan to hit within the year), moderate, or long-term. This will force you to be intentional about budgeting and also to follow through.

- *Pay down debt.* There are many different

approaches to this. You can pay down the largest debt amount first, the debt with the highest interest rate, or the smallest debts (working up to the largest). Some people like the momentum that they feel when knocking off a list of small debts. Just pick the approach that appeals to you and that you are most likely to stick to. The idea here is to get control of your debt before it becomes a burden.

- *Reward yourself within reason.* You deserve some fun and good times, but there must be a balance. If you want a big vacation, then you will have to figure out what you're going to give up to save for that vacation. The idea is to reward yourself within reason and not go into debt over material possessions or expensive experiences.

A Path for Growth

Many emerging professional leaders are more aware of money and their financial situation than previous generations were. One of the main drivers for this is student loan debt. This high, sometimes crippling debt has caused an entire generation of college graduates to hold off on buying homes and starting families. Perhaps you've experienced this first-hand.

The good news is that there is a way out. By negotiating your salary, saving for retirement, paying down debt, and holding off on reward purchases or budgeting wisely for them, you can implement a long-term strategy that will provide you with a comfortable, rewarding life as you continue to grow in your career, your skills, and your life. I have included a budget worksheet and a sample budget ratio, along with other resources, in Appendix A.

Chapter Ten Questions

Evaluate: What is your greatest frustration with your personal finances? What money mistakes have you made, and what financial decisions have you gotten right? What are your (realistic) financial goals for one, five, ten, and twenty years from now?

_____

_____

_____

_____

_____

_____

_____

_____

_____

_____

Take Action: Research what others in your field and location are making. Practice how you might negotiate for a higher salary or increased benefits, either at your next performance evaluation at your current job or at your next job.

Take Action: Work out a budget based on your current salary that allows you to meet expenses, save toward large purchases, pay off debt, and save for retirement. If all of these are not possible, brainstorm options, such as getting a second job or doing some freelance work on the side, changing your housing or transportation situation to cut down on expenses, or negotiating with your employer for a raise or help with student loans and an employee benefit.

Take Action: Take a personal finance course to get control of your money and make sure that you are making sound decisions for the best possible financial future. Consult Appendix A for further resources.

Chapter Ten Notes

_____

_____

_____

_____

_____

_____

_____

_____

_____

_____

_____

_____

_____

_____

_____

_____

_____

_____

_____

_____

_____

_____

_____

_____

CONCLUSION

Never Stop

It's time to own your career. It's time to stop being the passive worker, waiting for things to change on their own. *You are the agent of change for your life*, so stop procrastinating and take the initiative to go above and beyond.

It's time to reap the benefits of being able to mold your career into something that showcases your abilities and challenges your limits. It's time to make decisions, boldly explore the edge, and ask for forgiveness instead of permission.

If you invest in yourself, sharpen your skills and learn new ones, and become an authentic leader whom others can rely on, you will see growth and budding opportunities in your career. This is how you get promoted. This is how you map out your future.

Being promoted, however, is just the beginning. Anyone can be a manager, but it takes a very special person to be a respected coach and leader. Be the kind of person who praises others when praise is due and doesn't shy away from confrontation. Help others to realize their potential by coaching the best from them. Connect with your team on an individual basis as you strive to communicate clearly and effectively.

Never stop learning. Never stop seeking out mentors. Never stop networking. Learn how to make success, money, and assets work for you instead of control you.

All of this starts with awareness. Look around at work. What is your role? How do others see you? How do you want them to see you? Then act. Make the changes that are needed. Learn the skills. Forge the alliances.

Your future is in your hands now, from career to retirement. You have the tools. You have what it takes to get to *the next level.*

APPENDIX A

Recommended Resources

Resource for Chapter Three

The following resource provides valuable insights into successful networking:

- *The 20-Minute Network Meeting* by Nathan A. Perez and Marcia Ballinger (Career Innovations Press, 2015)

Resources for Chapter Four

The acronym GROW provides a representation of the four key components of the process of making a decision: goal, reality, options, and will or way forward. In what follows, we will take a closer look at each component.[18]

A Closer Look: Goal

Setting goals is a foundation of coaching. The first thing you must do to implement the GROW model is to identify a goal that you want to achieve. You can create a goal for something small, such as a conversation, or something much larger, such as an entire project or new role. Goals also vary by type and can be performance-based, development-based, relational-based, or to solve a problem or make a decision. Your goal at this point may be to become more coachable or to dare to make that first decision on your own without asking your superiors.

Once you've identified a goal, here are some questions to help clarify it:

- Why are you hoping to achieve this goal?

- What would be the benefits of achieving this goal?

- What will be different as a result of working on this?

- How can we make the goal measurable so that we know when you've achieved it?

- By when do you want to have this done?

- In X months, what do you want to have accomplished?

- What are the consequences if you do not reach this goal?

A Closer Look: Reality

Now that you have your goal, it's time to focus on the current reality. Getting the results you want won't be easy because there are usually many moving parts and many factors in achieving any given goal. Here are some questions to ask to assess the current reality of your goal:

- Briefly, what has been happening?

- What is the state of your project, your career, or the client relationship right now?

- What have you tried so far? What difference did those actions make?

- What factors do you think led you to this point?

- Which factors are most important in this?

- What do you view as obstacles for you? For others?

- In what different ways might others describe the situation?

- What else is important to know about the current situation?

- Is the goal still realistic?

A Closer Look: Options

Once the reality of the situation has been assessed, you should then focus on exploring ways to reach the goal.

- What are your options?

- What do you think you need to do next?

- What could be your first step?

- What else could you do?

- Who might be able to help you?

- What would happen if you did nothing?

- What is the hardest or most challenging part for you?

- What is the best thing and the worst thing about that option?

- What other potential course of action can you think of?

- Do any of these ideas interest you enough to explore them further?

- How have you approached a similar situation before?

- What could you do differently?

- What if this obstacle were removed? What would you do then?

- What could help you?

- If you were observing this conversation, what would you recommend?

- If other people are involved, what would they need to see or hear to get their attention?

- What have you seen others do that might work for you?

- If anything were possible, what might you do?
- Which option do you feel ready to act on?
- Whom can you ask for further suggestions?

A Closer Look: Will or Way Forward

The final step in the GROW model is to check your commitment level and then create a clear plan for concrete next steps. Here are questions to help confirm your commitment level:

- Which options do you want to pursue?
- What and when is the next step?
- What step can you take this week that will move you toward your goal?
- How are you going to go about it?
- What do you think you need to do right now? How are you going to do that?
- Is there anything else you can do?
- What resources can help you?
- What one small step will you take now?
- When are you going to start?
- What resources and/or support do you need to get that done?
- What do you need from others to help you achieve this?
- What are three actions you can take that would make sense this week?

- You mentioned that you could do _____.
  What will you commit to doing?

- How will you go about it?

- On a scale of one to ten, how committed and
  motivated are you to doing it? (If the answer is
  less than an eight, determine what would have
  to happen to make it a ten.)

Resources for Chapter Six

The following resources provide an in-depth look at thinking more productively:

- *Think Better: An Innovator's Guide to Productive Thinking* by Tim Hurson

- *Thinkertoys: A Handbook of Creative-Thinking Techniques* by Michael Michalko

The following resources will help you with time management:

- *Getting Things Done* by David Allen: This is a very comprehensive guide to productivity and organization. While the whole GTD system can be a game changer, simply trying Allen's two-minute rule is great for people who want to reduce messages that seem to linger in their inbox and make the most of those spare minutes before the next meeting. The two-minute rule states that if the next action can be done in two minutes or less, do it now, rather than deferring it to your to-do list.

- *The Pomodoro Technique*: Suitable for procrastinators and those who are easily distracted, this technique has you working intensely on a task for twenty-five minutes, after which is a five-minute break. Set a timer on your phone or try the site http://e.ggtimer.com/pomodoro.

- *Batch-Like Tasks*: Keep the momentum going by batching like tasks from different projects together. Writing, reading technical documents, or even phone calls can be batched and done in one focused session.

- *Reduce Your Distractions*: Try turning off your email and only checking it three times a day (unless your role requires you to reply to messages within a certain time for a service-level agreement), silencing your phone, isolating yourself by reserving a quiet room or wearing noise-canceling headphones, and closing your browser. Use only the apps or programs needed to do your task.

Suggested Reading:

- *Work Simply: Embracing the Power of Your Personal Productivity Style* by Carson Tate

- *Getting Things Done* by David Allen

- *Essentialism: The Disciplined Pursuit of Less* by Greg McKeown

- *Deep Work* by Cal Newport

Resources for Chapter Seven

Suggested Reading:

- "The Ladder of Inference (How Not to Jump to Conclusions)" (https://www.mindtools.com/pages/article/newTMC_91.htm)

- *Difficult Conversations: How to Discuss What Matters Most* by Douglas Stone and Bruce Patton

- *Crucial Conversations: Tools for Talking When Stakes Are High* by Kerry Patterson, Joseph Grenny, Ron McMillan, and Al Switzler

- *The Book of Beautiful Questions: The Powerful Questions That Will Help You Decide, Create, Connect, and Lead* by Warren Berger

Resource for Chapter Eight

The following resource provides a list of seven questions you can use to build coaching into your employee meetings:

- "7 Essential Questions All Great Managers Ask Their Employees," by Michael Bungay Stanier (https://www.businessinsider.com/questions-successful-managers-ask-employees-2016-3)

Resources for Chapter Nine

Meeting Calculators

- https://hbr.org/2016/01/estimate-the-cost-of-a-meeting-with-this-calculator

- https://www.calculators.org/business/meeting-costs.php

Reference Guide for Meetings

Things to do before the meeting:

- Define the purpose and desired outcome.

- Decide who should be in the room.

- Outline and send out a specific agenda that lists points to cover and time allotted in the meeting to cover them.

- Assign any tasks to be completed before the meeting (e.g. reading or work that must be accomplished for discussion within the meeting).

Things to do at the start of the meeting:

- Reiterate and confirm the purpose.

- Set the ground rules and confirm roles if needed.

- Move through the agenda based on the pre-determined schedule, keeping things on track.

- Manage the time and manage driving each agenda item through, keeping people on task.

Things to do after the meeting:

- Have the note taker send out the notes within two days of the meeting. As soon as possible is ideal. After two days, it is stale.

One-on-One Meetings

One-on-one meetings differ from team/group meetings and do require some regularity to balance employee autonomy and micromanaging. Here are some basic to-dos:

- Be consistent. Meet at least every month, but some employees will need once per week.

- Never miss a meeting if you can help it—definitely not more than two consecutive meetings. You may reschedule if necessary, but do not let that become a habit.

- Balance the agenda items and keep focus on the employee.

- Take notes to capture the most important info and to inform the next meeting.

How Do I Prepare?

Ask yourself these questions:

- What do my follow-up notes say that I need to check on?

- What do I need to be sure to communicate?

- What behavior of his or hers am I focusing on?

- What organization issues, news, and efforts can I share? What meetings have I just attended, and what did I learn? What are the common items I need to get out to everyone about schedules, projects, workload, or our team?

- What positive feedback can I give?

- What feedback can I give about what needs to be done differently?

- Is there something I can delegate? What project, task, or work would be helpful to the employee's development?

Sample Questions/Prompts to Ask the Employee

- Tell me about what you've been working on.

- What questions do you have about this project?

- Tell me about your week. What's it been like?

- Where do you think I can be most helpful?

- Tell me about your family, weekend, and activities.

- How are you going to approach this?

- Tell me about anything you stumbled over.

- What are your thoughts on my changes?

- Would you update me on Project X? What do you think about it?

- Are you on track to meet the deadline? What is helping or hindering the work?

- What questions do you have about the project?

- How do you think we can do this better?

- What are your future goals in this area?

- What areas of your work are you confident about? What are your plans to get there?

- What worries you? What can you or we do differently next time?

- Tell me about what you've learned on this project.

Coaching Meeting Agenda

Duration: Thirty Minutes

- Ten minutes for the employee's agenda items, such as project/work status updates or personal updates

- Ten minutes for the manager to share news, information, and updates on the team and organization

- Ten minutes for performance feedback and employee coaching for career/growth/development

Sample Agenda

1. Manager

- Follow up on items from the last meeting. What needs to be checked on?

- *The What*: Organizational or project updates (if not shared in a team meeting)

- *The So What*: Context or impact on the

employee of any organizational updates and changes

- *The Now What*: Next steps concerning the updates, if any. Do they impact the work or how decisions should be made?

- Ask the employee, "What should I stop, start, change, or continue doing that will help me to lead you effectively?"

2. Employee

- What the employee has been working on and results he or she has achieved in moving toward goals (likely focused on the top three priorities). What obstacles has he or she encountered? What wins should you recognize?

- Questions the employee has about the organization, the department, the work, the people, the tools, or the processes

- What the employee is planning to do in the time until the next one-on-one meeting

Suggested Reading:

- *No Fail Meetings: 5 Steps to Orchestrate Productive Meetings (and Avoid All the Rest)* by Michael Hyatt

Resources for Chapter Ten

I recommend the following resources about understanding and negotiating your salary:

- Georgetown University Center on Education and the Workforce. https://cew.georgetown.edu/good-jobs-project/.

- https://www.linkedin.com/salary/.

The following resource includes financial tips from University of Chicago professor Harold Pollack:

- Arnold, Chris. "Can The Best Financial Tips Fit On An Index Card?" *NPR*. January 8, 2016. https://www.npr.org/sections/alltechconsidered/2016/01/08/462250239/when-an-index-card-of-financial-tips-isnt-enough-this-book-is-there.

The following resource provides a budget worksheet from the FDIC:

- https://www.fdic.gov/consumers/assistance/protection/depaccounts/savings/savingsspending-plan-sample-income-and-expense-worksheet.pdf.

This is another good resource providing tips on how to budget:

- https://blog.mint.com/saving/how-to-budget/.

The following information provided by Dave Ramsey

clarifies household budget percentages:

- https://www.thewaystowealth.com/money-man-agement/household-budget-percentages/.

Acknowledgments

I would like to thank:

Caroline Barry—for your beta-reader advice and your perspective.

Courtney Barry—for brain picking and your perspective.

Alexis Borges—for caring for my children with love while I wrote this book.

Karen Burke—for being the mentor coach who shared her wise experience and perspectives.

Carson Burrington—for brain picking and your perspective.

Liz Cerrato—for help with Human Resources trends and for referring my work.

Melissa Christenson—for taking a chance on me in 2014 and for being such a fun travel buddy.

Debra Chromy—for trusting me with your clients and your overall encouragement.

Nina Coil—for sorting my original content outline and for being such a fabulous travel buddy.

Kelly Collins—for help with Human Resources trends and for trusting me to coach your leaders.

Tara Bridget Condon—for being my biggest cheerleader.

George Covino—for being an inspiring story in this book, for leading by example, and for teaching me to "plan your work and work your plan."

Sharon Currier—for your encouragement and great coaching

questions.

Joanne Dashiell—for being an empathetic manager and collaborator.

Juliann Decker—for your encouragement about becoming a coach.

Juliana Farrell—for being there at the beginning with encouragement.

Ann Farrell—for being a phenomenal business coach. When the student was ready, the teacher appeared!

Patrice Fogg—for your support and encouragement.

Meagan Foy—for brain picking and for supporting a fellow Bentley Falcon!

Martha Frost—for your support and encouragement.

Ellen Gillis—for brain picking and for trusting me to facilitate in your organization.

Mitchell Gordon—for creating the first graphic for my consulting brand and choosing the color orange for me.

Moira Keating—for brain picking on Human Resources and for trusting me to coach your valuable leaders.

Marguerite Kerr—for help with Human Resources trends and for trusting me to coach your leaders.

Michael Kradas—for brain picking and for letting me loose on the Leadership Academy.

Carol Lucente—for giving me the foundation of a great education, both at home and at Bentley.

Donna Lucente—for your support and for spoiling my kids.

Victoria Lucente-Bonadio and family—for your support and for spoiling my kids.

Sabrina Mainini—for your valuable feedback on my first chapter.

Rachel Mandina—for saying, "Of course you are!" when I told you that I was writing a book.

Sarah Mann—for your encouragement and for creating the

WGT network of mighty women.

Andrew Marley—my "work husband." I miss noodling ideas on the whiteboard with you. Thank you for encouraging me.

Betsy Mayotte—for your encouragement.

Michael McDonough—for not laughing at me when I ask about tax breaks for my unusual business expenses.

Kim Menninger—for your encouragement.

Susan Nathan—for setting the bar for the client experience and for being the one who warned others about the "red lights."

Ryan Newman—for brain picking and sharing your perspective as an emerging leader.

Bill Pasnau—for being a great guide and for the most kooky virtual meetings.

Kara Puffer—for your support and encouragement.

Sarah Puleo—for your editing and messaging prowess.

Imisa Sanchez—for your encouragement and accountability.

Eric Savickas—for tossing around ideas and for your encouragement.

Doug Schaeffer—for your perspective as a business leader and your kind and encouraging words.

Jennifer Schott—for your support and for keeping me on my toes for inbox containment.

J. Andrew Shepardson, Ph.D.—for your opinion on setting expectations and for helping a Bentley University.

Zoe Silverman—for brain picking and for trusting me to facilitate in your organization.

Jonathan Sparling—for writing the money chapter and for being a collaborative colleague.

Amy Tananbaum—for the great opportunities to facilitate and to coach your clients.

Tracy Terry—for brain picking and for trusting me to facilitate in your organization.

James Turk—for trusting me with your clients and for

facilitation and coaching.

Claudyne Wilder—for trusting me with your clients and your excellent workshop content.

Justine Wirtanen—for your support and encouragement.

Kimberly Woolridge—for your encouraging words and grammar skills.

The Cupp Family—for being my biggest fans. Do I have you fooled or what?

Laurel Grove Shop—for my space to write and for the great water-cooler chat.

About the Author

Gina Lucente-Cole is an expert in career accelerators. She guides emerging leaders to become more visible for their contribution and rise in their careers.

She also helps organizations to improve performance through her expertise in organizational development, team facilitation, performance consulting, and leadership development workshops and coaching.

Her clients include public companies, private firms, and non-profit organizations in the business, science, service, financial, and educational industries.

Learn more at www.ProminaAdvisors.com.

About Speak It To Book

Speak It to Book, the premier ghostwriting agency and publisher for thought leaders, is revolutionizing how books are created and used.

We are a team of people who are passionate about making your great ideas famous.

Imagine:

- What if you had a way to beat writer's block, overcome your busy schedule, and get all of those ideas out of your head?

- What if you could partner with a team to crush lack of motivation and productivity so you can get your story in front of the people who need it most?

- What if you took that next step into significance and influence, using your book to launch your platform?

- What if you could write your book with a team of professionals from start to finish?

Your ideas are meant for a wider audience. Visit www.speakittobook.com to schedule a call with our team of publishing professionals today.

REFERENCES

Notes

[1] Drucker, Peter. *The Effective Executive*. Harper & Row, 1967.

[2] Schabner, Dean. "Americans: Overworked, Overstressed." Web.archive.org. July 12, 2018. https://web.archive.org/web/20180712005103/https:/abcnews.go.com/US/story?id=93604&page=1.

[3] Garton, Eric. "Employee Burnout Is a Problem with the Company, Not the Person." Harvard Business Review. April 6, 2017. https://hbr.org/2017/04/employee-burnout-is-a-problem-with-the-company-not-the-person.

[4] Allen, David. *Ready for Anything: 52 Productivity Principles for Getting Things Done*. New York: Penguin Books, 2003.

[5] Peters, Tom. "The Brand Called You." Fast Company. August 31, 1997. https://www.fastcompany.com/28905/brand-called-you.

[6] Von Moltke, Helmuth. "On Strategy." 1871. In *Moltke on the Art of War*. Translated by Daniel J. Hughes and Harry Bell.

Presidio Press, 1993, p. 92.

[7] Peters, Kim, and Alex Haslam. "Research: To Be a Good Leader, Start by Being a Good Follower." Harvard Business Review. August 6, 2018. https://hbr.org/2018/08/research-to-be-a-good-leader-start-by-being-a-good-follower.

[8] Fine, Alan, with Rebecca R. Merrill. *You Already Know How to Be Great: A Simple Way to Remove Interference and Unlock Your Greatest Potential* (Ch. 4). Portfolio/Penguin, 2010.

[9] Burkus, David. "Some Companies Are Banning Email and Getting More Done." Harvard Business Review. June 8, 2016. https://hbr.org/2016/06/some-companies-are-banning-email-and-getting-more-done.

[10] Harrell, Melissa, and Lauren Barbato. "Great Managers Still Matter: The Evolution of Google's Project Oxygen." re:Work. February 27, 2018. https://rework.withgoogle.com/blog/the-evolution-of-project-oxygen/.

[11] Michalko, Michael. *Thinkertoys: A Handbook of Creative-Thinking Techniques*. New York: Random House, 2006.

[12] De Bono, Edward. "Six Thinking Hats." The De Bono Group. http://www.debonogroup.com/six_thinking_hats.php.

[13] Allen, David. "When Office Technology Overwhelms, Get Organized." *The New York Times*. March 17, 2012. https://www.nytimes.com/2012/03/18/business/when-office-technology-overwhelms-get-organized.html.

[14] Clear, James. "How to Be More Productive and Eliminate Time Wasting Activities by Using the 'Eisenhower Box.'" Jamesclear.com. https://jamesclear.com/eisenhower-box.

[15] Delong, Thomas. "Three Questions for Effective Feedback." Harvard Business Review. August 4, 2011. https://hbr.org/2011/08/three-questions-for-effective-feedback.

[16] Cleaver, Joanne. "Meetings and Team Management." Sage Business Researcher. March 14, 2016. https://jycleaver.com/wp-content/uploads/2012/05/Meetings-%E2%80%93-SAGE-Business-Cleaver-.compressed.pdf.

[17] Cleaver, "Meetings and Team Management."

[18] Fine and Merrill, *You Already Know How to Be Great.*

Made in the USA
Columbia, SC
27 November 2020